P9-CBD-490

MORE PRAISE FOR *LEADING CHANGE STEP-BY-STEP*

"Jody Spiro offers us a gift in making clear that change is possible and then—drawing on both her field experience and her teaching—lays out in clear and concise ways the tools leaders need to achieve the change they seek."

—**Ellen Schall,** dean, Robert F. Wagner Graduate
School of Public Service, New York University

"Jody Spiro's first-hand expert knowledge of change management provides step-by-step insights on the multiple forces affecting project, organizational, and system change across the educational sector. Her wide-ranging command of principles and best practices are in evidence in every example and case that she tracks from concept through full implementation. Every manager should read this wise and superbly crafted handbook of organizational change."

—**Dan E. Davidson,** president, American Councils
for International Education

"Jody Spiro has captured the essence of leading change. By providing useful tactics, tools, and tales of the adventures of organizations that have realized dynamic systemic change, she guides readers from the first gleam in the eye of the leader who envisions a different organization through the essentials of maintaining the achieved changes. Unless you are dedicated to maintaining the status quo in your organization, you must read this book!"

—**Phillip S. Rogers, Ed.D.,** executive director,
Education Professional Standards Board

"Jody Spiro's book is essential reading for any social sector leader facing transition and uncertainty. Leaders will become more agile and adaptive thanks to the powerful roadmaps, easy-to-use tools, and concrete examples of what organizations must do to remain relevant in an era of declining resources and rising expectations."

—**Beryl Levinger,** Distinguished Professor and Chair of the Public
Administration Program at the Monterey Institute of
International Studies, a Graduate School of Middlebury College

"Dr. Spiro knows of what she speaks. Her national and international work has served her well as she has prepared a down-to-earth and research-sound process for leading change. This book is not about responding to change, it is about leading change; it is a guide for us to be proactive as opposed to our always being reactive to the constant change around us."

—**Dr. William Callahan**, professor and Dean Emeritus, University of Northern Iowa

"Dr. Spiro's remarkable work Leading Change Step-by-Step *is a must for the social work profession. It is both relevant and pertinent to social workers working as agents of change in Macro practice, administration, the establishment of public policy, and the enactment of legislation. Simultaneously, it is perfect for the Micro practitioner working with individuals, couples, families, and organizations. As a social work educator, I highly recommend it to my fellow academicians for use in the classroom.*"

—**Dr. Cheryl Resnick-Cortes,** chair and Program Director of Social Work, Georgian Court University

"Jody Spiro has the unique combination of practical leadership experience in different countries and many years of working with theory. That makes the book the real practical guide how to lead change."

—**Dr. Elena Karpukhina**, vice rector, Academy of National Economy under the Government of Russian Federation

"This book is an insightful reflection of Dr. Spiro's work with the agents of change around the world. Government officials, managers, teachers, and practitioners in my country will benefit from the tactics and tools but will also discover the essence of their own tale."

—**Otilia Ştefania Păcurari**, Prof. I dr., National Institute for Magistracy, Romania, and international education consultant

"Leaders in any type of organization will benefit from the information provided. Change is critical in public education today, and the tools and tactics discussed in this book will allow leaders to successfully deploy new initiatives, projects and/or programs."

—**Joe Simpson,** Deputy State Superintendent of Public Instruction, State of Wyoming Department of Education

"The need for change in education has never been greater, along with leaders who can articulate a shared vision and organize the resources—human, fiscal, and organizational—necessary to achieve it. This book lays out the steps leaders must take to foster and sustain real change. Its field-tested tools and tales from the front lines of leading change are more than a "how-to" course in organizational leadership in challenging times, they provide an inspiring vision for educational transformation, and a road map for the continuous journey of innovation and discovery that change leadership demands."

—**David Haselkorn,** associate commissioner,
MA Department of Elementary and Secondary Education

"This book provides important information that is helpful to any leader of change as well as tools and strategies that are specific to educators. In the current era of school reform, it is a valuable step-by-step resource to not only implement change but also to sustain it."

—**Dr. Wendy Robinson**, superintendent,
Fort Wayne Community Schools, Fort Wayne, Indiana

"Starting a voyage toward change is one thing. Successfully reaching the destination is another. Jody Spiro's Leading Change Step-by-Step *serves as an essential guidebook for education leaders as they journey from planning for change, to securing stakeholder support, to implementing and sustaining strategic reforms. Jody brings together some of the best thinking and hands-on tools to help education leaders understand the full spectrum of a change process and to become more skillful in leading, managing, and engaging people in change. I have used her work over the years in moving forward systemic change in my role as superintendent in Eugene."*

—**George Russell**, superintendent,
Eugene School District 4J, Eugene, Oregon

"Jody Spiro expands our thinking and captures the critical elements of the role of leadership in setting the stage and creating the conditions for moving an agenda that demands both equity and excellence."

—**Dr. Carol Johnson**, superintendent, Boston Public Schools

"A must read for new and veteran administrators and managers. Not only is it well organized and easy to follow, but, it has well researched step-by-step directions on avoiding the pitfalls many new and veteran administrators and managers wish they had considered."

—**Paulina A. Ugo**, principal, Park View
Elementary School, Victorville, CA.

"Jody Spiro makes the important point that change is constant, and that it consists of a million moving parts. Leading Change Step-by-Step, *gives leaders the essential tools they need to manage the motion of those moving parts."*

—Paul J. Thompson, founding principal,
Urban Assembly School of Music and Art, Brooklyn, New York

"Leading change is an intentional and dynamic process requiring leaders of complex systems to plan for, be aware of, and reflect on the effects of their decisions, plans, and attitudes on real people. Dr. Spiro's work beautifully and accessibly shares the process that any thoughtful service leader will want to employ when considering the acceleration of progress of people-serving systems."

—Joseph Scantlebury, Esq., attorney and Education
Equity Advocate, Washington DC

"Teacher Leaders who use Jody Spiro's Leading Change *tools will be equipped to face challenges in a proactive, responsive manner as they engage their school community in improving teaching and learning."*

—Karyn S. Rosenfield, teacher leader,
Providence Public Schools, Providence RI

"Jody Spiro offers a clear, concise, and cogent summary of change theory and the protocols and tools that make significant and dramatic change possible and effective. Both veteran and new leaders of change will find much to pique their enthusiasm, energize their resolve, and enhance their expertise."

—James C. Lalley, Ed.D., executive leadership
coach, Chicago Public Schools

"Jody Spiro has provided a critical guide that enables the reader to focus on making conscious and intentional changes in their environments. Whether an emerging or accomplished leader, the practical tools provided are an excellent conceptual map to making complex, resistant change successful."

—Andy Cole, director, Leadership Development,
Fairfax County Public Schools, Fairfax VA

Leading Change Step-by-Step

Leading Change Step-by-Step
Tactics, Tools, and Tales

Jody Spiro

JOSSEY-BASS
A Wiley Imprint
www.josseybass.com

Copyright © 2011 by John Wiley & Sons, Inc. All rights reserved.

Published by Jossey-Bass
A Wiley Imprint
989 Market Street, San Francisco, CA 94103-1741—www.josseybass.com

No part of this publication may be reproduced, stored in a retrieval system, or transmitted in any form or by any means, electronic, mechanical, photocopying, recording, scanning, or otherwise, except as permitted under Section 107 or 108 of the 1976 United States Copyright Act, without either the prior written permission of the publisher, or authorization through payment of the appropriate per-copy fee to the Copyright Clearance Center, Inc., 222 Rosewood Drive, Danvers, MA 01923, 978-750-8400, fax 978-646-8600, or on the Web at www.copyright.com. Requests to the publisher for permission should be addressed to the Permissions Department, John Wiley & Sons, Inc., 111 River Street, Hoboken, NJ 07030, 201-748-6011, fax 201-748-6008, or online at www.wiley.com/go/permissions.

Readers should be aware that Internet Web sites offered as citations and/or sources for further information may have changed or disappeared between the time this was written and when it is read.

Limit of Liability/Disclaimer of Warranty: While the publisher and author have used their best efforts in preparing this book, they make no representations or warranties with respect to the accuracy or completeness of the contents of this book and specifically disclaim any implied warranties of merchantability or fitness for a particular purpose. No warranty may be created or extended by sales representatives or written sales materials. The advice and strategies contained herein may not be suitable for your situation. You should consult with a professional where appropriate. Neither the publisher nor author shall be liable for any loss of profit or any other commercial damages, including but not limited to special, incidental, consequential, or other damages.

Jossey-Bass books and products are available through most bookstores. To contact Jossey-Bass directly call our Customer Care Department within the U.S. at 800-956-7739, outside the U.S. at 317-572-3986, or fax 317-572-4002.

Jossey-Bass also publishes its books in a variety of electronic formats. Some content that appears in print may not be available in electronic books.

Library of Congress Cataloging-in-Publication Data
Spiro, Jody.
  Leading change step-by-step : tactics, tools, and tales / by Jody Spiro.
      p. cm.
  Includes index.
  ISBN 978-0-470-63562-9 (pbk.)
  ISBN 978-0-470-91525-7 (ebk.)
  ISBN 978-0-470-91526-4 (ebk.)
  ISBN 978-0-470-91527-1 (ebk.)
  1. Educational leadership. 2. Educational change. 3. Educational innovations. I. Title.
  LB2806.S652 2011
  371.2'07—dc22
                                 2010023123

Printed in the United States of America
FIRST EDITION
PB Printing 10 9 8 7 6 5 4 3 2 1

CONTENTS

Dedicated to the many colleagues in many places who have been using these tools and inspiring me with their accomplishments

ACKNOWLEDGMENTS

This book has been many years in the making. It was born of a sense that there are several useful techniques for leading change that could be translated into tools to assist busy leaders. These techniques reflect, and have their roots in, a rich body of thinking in this field as well as my own career experiences. This includes work I began as head of professional development for the operations department at Chase Manhattan Bank and continued through senior management stints in the public, nonprofit, university, foundation, and international development sectors. Throughout my career, I have shared the lessons I was learning with my graduate students at New York University's Wagner Graduate School of Public Service. Over more than 18 years, my students have used versions of these tools and materials. Most recently, during my work at The Wallace Foundation, many state and district leaders participating in the Foundation's education leadership initiative have used these tactics and tools as they pursue lasting change in their education systems.

The ideas and views expressed in this book are mine alone. However, many people have helped along the way. A number of colleagues from across the United States and in other countries as well have made this work come alive with vivid examples. They include: Lois Adams-Rodgers, Victor Bolotov, Joanne Brady, Vladimir Briller, Andrew Cole, Debbie Daniels, Ann Duffy, Larry Finkel, Troyce Fisher, Simon Fenster, Pamela Ferner, Lucia Gliga, Bonnie Gross, Mall Hellum, Roberta Hendee, Erika Hunt, Ronald Israel, Elena Karpuhina, Judith Monseur, Kathleen Nadurak, Ed Miley, Otilia Pacurari, Linda Roman, Robert Santa Morena, John Schoener, Mark Shellinger, Sheila Smith-Anderson, Ann Southworth, Sandra Stein, Marina Vildziuniene, Casel Walker, Lynne Wheat, Jackie O. Wilson, and Cynthia Yoder. Their thoughtful reflections on the tools and tactics through the years have been invaluable.

I would especially like to acknowledge and thank my colleagues at The Wallace Foundation. In particular, Richard Laine has long supported using these tactics and tools to accelerate the important work of Wallace education leadership grantees. Lee Mitgang encouraged me and served as editor for an earlier iteration. Lucas Held and Ayeola Boothe-Kinlaw generously reviewed drafts of this book and provided valuable feedback. Special thanks are also due to Marjorie McAneny, my editor at Jossey-Bass, who, in approaching this work with fresh eyes and expertise, contributed her own perspectives that led to further improvement.

And, finally, thanks to my wonderful, longtime friends: Abby, Alberto, Cheryl, Cindy, Gay, Jessica, Linda, and Lisa, who were always there when I needed a break from writing!

ABOUT THE AUTHOR

JODY SPIRO, ED.D., has worked with schools, districts, nonprofits and governments in the U.S. and abroad on leading change. She currently serves as adjunct professor at NYU's Wagner Graduate School of Public Service and as a senior program officer at The Wallace Foundation where she works with education leaders across the United States.

Prior to joining The Wallace Foundation, Dr. Spiro held leadership positions at large organizations in the private, public, nonprofit, university, philanthropic, and international sectors. She has seen firsthand that the approach laid out in this book applies in all these venues.

Dr. Spiro presents frequently on the topic of leading change at conferences held by organizations such as: ASCD, The National Staff Development Council, The National Council of State Legislatures, The National Association of State Boards of Education, The Council of Chief State School Officers, and The Wallace Foundation.

Leading Change Step-by-Step

The Essentials of Leading Change Step-by-Step

Because I took the necessary time to go through the steps outlined in the tools my staff is embracing the change instead of resisting it as "one more thing."

—An elementary school principal

These tools support us to be intentional about including important components of leading change. They help us not to make assumptions. The implementation is in its earliest stages, but there is a buzz across the district. The change tools engage people at every level of the organization. They help predict behaviors and prevent mistakes that could be time stealers to implementation, and they monitor progress so we can make mid-course corrections. Knowing the process of change, and utilizing the tools, will keep our district from adding this initiative to all the many others that had a start, but no follow through. There will be sustainability.

—A district leader

The subject of leading change is of paramount importance for leaders these days as it seems that, more than ever, the only *constant* is change. Change can be deliberate or random—it can mean any departure from the status quo. But for the purposes of this book, change is assumed to be an intentional process toward the goal of meaningful, positive reform. Leadership is an essential ingredient in determining whether the process is successful.

Change involves going from one situation to another, which necessarily includes a period of transition. Change is a continuous process. Therefore, it can perhaps best be considered as a series of destinations that lead to further destinations. The change leader can use these destinations as benchmark goals and as indicators of success at various intervals, making course corrections as needed.

FIVE PREREQUISITES FOR CHANGE

Although every situation will be unique, there are common dynamics to leading change. If these are understood from the beginning, leaders will have a head start on success.

Understanding the Dynamics

Change can be a dynamic and positive force for creating new strategies and putting them into action, stimulating creativity, diversity, learning, and growth. But change of the sort discussed in this book also includes a deliberate disruption of the status quo. Although the need for change will often be apparent to many or most of those affected, opposition, resistance, and unanticipated consequences are all likely to emerge. These must be taken into account during planning and implementation. Even positive change can be stressful. An effective change leader can maximize the opportunities of change while minimizing the risks.

Unfortunately, many change efforts fail or are less successful than originally conceived. This is not surprising for the following reasons: unforeseen circumstances are likely to arise, participants may feel uncertain and unprepared for what is to come, stakeholders may oppose disruption of their current influence, or people may feel disempowered. There can be no guarantee of success up front. By definition, all change—even positive change—involves loss of what was and a transition to what will be. Even changes that you look forward to are stressful—just ask any bride, groom, or new parent!

Leading change therefore requires being intentional about analyzing the existing situation up front and then planning for, implementing, and continuously improving the change strategies and how you will achieve them. Leading change requires continuous analysis of the situation and midcourse corrections. In these ways, you can deal effectively with the unintended consequences that emerge: mitigating the negative consequences and embracing the positives. Both will inevitably happen.

Leading change also requires the ability to think several steps ahead and then plan the near future with the long term in mind. The type of change we seek is not incremental—not just a little more for a few more people or a little tinkering around the edges. It starts with a vision of the future and plans backward, rather than starting with what is and planning from there.

Leading change requires effective leaders to be reflective at all phases of the experience—before embarking, during the implementation, and beyond—and to make midcourse corrections along the way. Of course, continuous improvement requires analysis of what is not working well in order to improve things. But, less frequently done, it also requires critically analyzing what *is* working in order to determine if it will keep working in the future. The leader always has to keep an eye on the future while operating in the present. Even if something is working today, the question should be asked: is it likely to continue working effectively in the future?

Yes, leading change is complex. Yet it can be well managed by breaking it down into a series of practical steps that enable the leader to be intentional about each tactic. When led step-by-step, the result becomes more than the sum of the parts.

Using Multiple Perspectives

One of the keys to leading change is to examine everything through several lenses. Since you cannot be sure of the outcome, you better your odds of success by considering a variety of perspectives, particularly those different from your own, and testing assumptions.

We all like to think that our way of looking at the world is the "real" perspective. In truth, it represents only one view—yours. And it is most important to realize that your perspective is meaningful only to you. Change is a highly personal experience; everyone has different feelings about it. It is important to analyze your own views and feelings, but just as important to recognize that others probably do not share them.

Effective leaders deliberately seek out those whose views and values differ from their own in order to gain perspectives that they would not consider otherwise. It is critical when leading change for the leader to understand, be able to distinguish, and incorporate the following three perspectives into any change strategy:

- His or her own points of view

- The perspective of key implementers of the change strategy

- The prevailing culture of the organization

Understanding and incorporating these three distinctive sets of perspectives and values is essential to planning and implementing successful change and are therefore incorporated in the tools found in this book.

Making Strategic Decisions—and Backing Them Up in Action

The hardest part of leading change for many is that the leader has to consider and choose from a variety of reasonable options. This means privileging some work over other work and reallocating resources from lower priorities to the new. Some people and groups are more important to engage than others; some programs are more worthy of funding; some components of the work are non-negotiable. You need to be able to lead a process that identifies these priorities and puts them into action—even though other people, groups, and lower-priority programs will be affected.

Asking the Right Questions—and Taking the Time to Answer Them

Whether you are at the beginning of the planning process or trying to make a midcourse correction, there are several key questions you need to address:

- How can we ensure that what is planned will be well implemented and achieve the original purpose?

- What is the best way to start? How can we enter the process at any stage if we cannot choose our starting point?

- How can we keep getting better at what we do and build those improvements into subsequent plans?

- What would scale and sustainability look like?

- What steps can we build into our planning and implementation to increase the likelihood of sustaining the desired change and expanding its reach?

Leaders and their teams are busy people who frequently say, "We don't have the time for lengthy discussions." But, indeed, the discussions are essential—at the beginning and throughout the process. The time you devote up front will pay off later on. The tactics, tools, and tales in this book facilitate those discussions and analyses. Knowing the right questions to ask helps focus those conversations so that they take less time and are more productive.

WHAT YOU WILL FIND IN THIS BOOK

This book concentrates on a series of broad tactics that are essential for leading change. Frequently overlooked due to lack of awareness or time constraints, each is essential to securing the change you are after.

The Eight Steps

Step 1: Determine your change strategy.

After you determine the change strategy that will give you the biggest domino effect, you must define it specifically, including benchmarks and time lines.

Step 2: Assess readiness.

Once you set about trying to make change happen, you need to assess and improve the readiness of all parties to bring it about.

Step 3: Analyze the stakeholders.

It is then essential to understand the motivations of external stakeholders and know which groups are crucial to engage.

Step 4: Minimize resistance.

An effective change leader attempts to minimize the inevitable resistance from affected individuals and assesses his or her own tolerance for any resistance that will be engendered nevertheless.

Step 5: Secure a small early win.

Once the design elements have been developed to engage the internal and external groups, it is very helpful to plan and secure a small "early win" that will convince everyone that the change strategy is desirable and feasible.

Step 6: Engage the key players in planning.

The skillful bringing together of all internal and external players in collaborative planning will further define the action steps needed to achieve the change strategy without watering down the original aims.

Step 7: Scale and sustain the change strategy.

It is also essential to comprehensively plan and implement ways to scale and sustain the initiative over time.

Step 8: Build in ongoing monitoring and course corrections.

The last step in leading change is to reflect on whether the change strategy indeed solved the original problem. Many times leaders only assess whether the strategy was well implemented—and not whether the strategy actually addressed the original goal. Because the result of your change strategy cannot be guaranteed, and change is constant and continuous, these analyses must be used in an ongoing way. The work is never finished.

Tactics: Essential Elements and Mistakes to Avoid

Within those broad concepts, several essential elements are discussed. Those descriptions contain not only effective practice, but also what can go wrong and how to avoid making common mistakes.

Field-Tested Tools

A missing ingredient for many practitioners has been how to translate concepts into action, continuous improvement, and sustainable results. Having a set of tools at hand can prevent common problems. Leaders often don't realize that what they are leading is change, with its own unique dynamics that must be taken into consideration.

One common issue is that leaders and their teams tend to "rush in," to propose implementing solutions to problems and not take the time to analyze the critical variables that will lead to success or failure. For example, they may not fully ascertain how ready the people and organization are for a change, who is likely to oppose and resist, or how even a successful venture can be sustained.

As a leader of change, you will need not only to develop strategies, but also to project what will happen to various other parts of the system as a result. It is clearly desirable to plan for change at the beginning of an initiative and use the model presented in this book step-by-step; however, you can enter the change process at any point as long as you recognize the dynamics of the change process and have the tools at hand.

The following table presents an overview of the change process, including what tools in this book correspond to which action step.

TACTICS	TOOLS
1. Determine your change strategy and make your plan	Strategy/Action Aligner
2. Assess and improve the readiness of those affected	Readiness Rubrics (for leader, participants, organization)
3. Analyze the stakeholders	Stakeholder Strategizer
4. Minimize resistance (and maximize your tolerance for it)	Resistance Reducer
5. Secure a small, early win	Early Win Wonder
6. Engage all those affected in collaborative planning	Collaborative Planning Parameters
7. Scale and sustain the initiative	Scale and Sustainability Score Sheet
8. Build in ongoing monitoring and continuous improvement	The 3 R's: Review, Revise, Repeat

■   ■   ■

Users of the tools have also found it useful to pull them out when they get stuck in their change processes. It is good to know that at whatever point you hit a roadblock, you can find a tool to help get the process moving productively again.

The following comments are typical from users:

Although the tools were useful at the beginning of the project to define goals, objectives, outcomes and strategies, they were also useful throughout the life of the project.

Using the tools in the middle of the process is essential because people change all the time and the new voices need to be heard.

The tools are designed to be usable and accessible; they represent not a single theory of change, but the best thinking from among those who write about the topic, synthesized from the many leaders who have used the tools in this book for the past several years, and from the author's own experience.

Every tool contains reflective questions for the leader that you might use to think through your personal reactions to change. This step is crucial. Your responses must be carefully and honestly thought out and supported by evidence; otherwise they are merely untested assumptions or what you might *like* to think about yourself as opposed to what really *is*.

Several tools use numeric scales within descriptors. These numbers have no statistical significance; they are used to help illustrate and calibrate your assessments on the items described. When numeric scales are used, they tally to 100 points (and therefore 100 percent) to help you understand more intuitively what the numbers mean. These numeric ratings are meant to help you in your assessment, not to imply statistical validity.

Tales of Struggle and Success

Leaders from twenty-two states and several countries have used versions of these tools during the past several years and have been generous to share the stories of their experiences. The anecdotes and cases that comprise the "tales" in this book reflect the composite experiences of these colleagues and the author. They reflect the stories of leaders of states large and small; of cities, suburbs, and rural areas; and of nonprofit organizations, both domestic and international. The lessons they illustrate therefore have a universality of application to all these settings and organization types in the public and nonprofit sectors.

For purposes of illustrating the leading change tactics, leaders' stories have been synthesized into composites—for example, the stories of organizations from different parts of the country that engaged in similar change strategies have been woven together to be more generally representative. However, the stories are all true and have not been altered to better illustrate the tactics they address.

We will follow tales from four hypothetical organizations:

- International Health and Human Services (IHHS)—a large, established human services organization with clients around the globe

- Talent Unlimited Inc. (TUI)—a small nonprofit consulting organization

- Changeville—a midsize school district

- Turnaround School—a pre-K–12 school in the Changeville district

Both the district and school include a synthesis of urban, rural, and suburban schools across all grade levels. The domestic and international organizations, similarly, work with clients of various sizes and locales.

The names of these composite organizations are intended to be fictitious. Any organizations having a similar name is a coincidence.

The stories illustrate the tactics and tools in the book, and include such examples as how:

- Organizations have developed large-scale reform in the United States and other countries, for revamping policies and institutions delivering teacher training countrywide.

- States have designed and implemented comprehensive education reform strategies.

- School districts and schools have developed leadership teams and professional learning communities, developed and implemented new curricula, and implemented programs to reduce the student dropout rate.

IT'S THE DESTINATION—NOT THE JOURNEY

When implementing a change effort, don't be surprised if your original strategy changes or if aspects of the work turn out differently than planned. It's entirely possible that what you end up doing is actually *better* than what you planned originally.

As long as the goal of the change is specific, clear, and nonnegotiable, the tactics may lead to different—and more effective—roads to achieving the goal. What is important is that the goal is achieved—and in a way that results in buy-in on the part of the stakeholders, affected individuals, and the organizational culture, for that is the only way that the strategy will be sustained.

To achieve a sustainable strategy, the leader must be clear and intentional about the change process, specific about the goals, open to better strategies to achieve the goals—and must continuously reassess all aspects of the change process as the work proceeds. If the change is well led, the result should make additional changes necessary—indeed, you will reach a series of destinations that lead to further destinations.

> Note that many of the forms in this book can be downloaded for free from the Jossey-Bass Web site. See appendix for instructions.

Determining Your Change Strategy—

and Making Your Plan

We thought we knew what we were doing until we started using the tools. Then we had to reconsider our strategies.

—A district leader

TACTICS

Although it is not the purpose of this book to describe strategic planning in any depth, it is necessary to begin here because before one can lead change, it must be clear what strategy is being pursued. It is essential that the leader be clear about what problem needs to be solved, the overall approach ("strategy") that should address this problem, how that strategy relates to the organization's core purpose, and the thinking behind why it should work.

The strategy should be one that is aspirational yet achievable and high leverage—meaning that by successfully implementing this one strategy it is likely that others will be accomplished as well. And, because change is a long-term prospect (a "series of destinations that lead to other destinations") the leader must determine what success would look like and which milestones should be used to measure it along the way. It should be transparent whether the actions that implement the strategy are on track or whether course corrections may be necessary.

Strategic planning is a systemic process through which an organization agrees upon and builds commitment to priorities that are crucial to its mission and are responsive to the environment. It is necessary to distinguish between what is essential to do and what is merely desirable to do.

It is therefore important to begin with an explicit understanding of the organization's mission and values and how those relate to the external environment (the larger economy, politics, and competing organizations, for example).

Strategic planning thus involves making choices. It is as much about what you will *not* do as what you will do. It is about choosing specific priorities, allocating resources, and focusing on what is really important to the organization's long-term success. Strategic planning is *continuous*. It emphasizes the development of approaches based on an assessment of both the organization's internal capacity and the external environment in which it functions. This facilitates not only strategy development, but also allocation of resources.

Essential Elements

Being aware of the main aspects of plan development can clarify your thinking and expedite the development of your change strategies. From developing the mission statement through designing strategies to accomplish it, here are some underlying elements that need to be thought through.

The Mission Statement

A mission statement usually describes the ultimate result that the organization is trying to accomplish and answers the questions, what is the organization's purpose? and what is it trying to achieve? The mission further pinpoints the need that the organization fills in the marketplace. It articulates the mandate (if there is one) and expands on it to create value beyond what the organization is charged with doing. And, finally, the mission statement usually explains how the organization goes about accomplishing its ends.

Internal Negotiations of the Mission Statement

It should be noted that the development of mission statements is best done by collaborative planning within an organization (see the Collaborative Planning Parameters in Step 6). You want a mission statement that truly represents the best thinking of the main players. Sometimes this means engaging in negotiations between and among different divisions as they develop their own mission statements aligned with that of the overall organization.

Mission Statements from Our Composite Organizations

As described in the Introduction, the four organizations that we will be following represent composites of like organizations pursuing similar goals. Their respective missions are described as follows:

Mission Statements of Our Four Organizations

International Health and Human Services, Inc. (IHHS)

For more than twenty years, IHHS has been a leader in international development. We advance learning, arts participation, and health for individuals of all ages around the world. The organization's work includes K–12 education for leaders, teachers and children, health promotion, use of technology, as well as encouraging participation in the arts. We build knowledge and skills by working collaboratively with local partners to engage learners as active, problem-solving participants.

Talent Unlimited, Inc. (TUI)

Founded in 1995, TUI recognizes and supports the important contributions made by nonprofit organizations in our city. We are committed to enhancing their human capital capacity to fulfill their respective missions. We do this through organizing ongoing training programs in leadership and service management as well as providing consultation to agencies, organizations, and individual leaders.

Changeville Public School District

The district exists to educate all students so that they have the skills they need to be productive citizens of the twenty-first century. Beyond academic learning, the district's mission is to ensure that each student fulfills his or her full potential and receives the services needed to do so. We accomplish this by providing supervision and support to twenty early childhood and elementary schools, five middle schools, and three high schools—all of which form an integrated system of learning. The district ensures the safety of its students and the seamlessness of their education between and among grade levels. All services are provided from pre-kindergarten through high school both before and after the school day.

Turnaround School

This Pre-K–12 school exists to educate all students so that they have the skills they need to be productive citizens of the twenty-first century. Beyond academic learning, the school's mission is to ensure that each student fulfills his or her full potential and receives the services needed to do so. We achieve this by providing the finest academic programs that are continuously updated as well as extracurricular activities such as sports and clubs and services such as health and nutrition. All services are provided both before and after the school day.

Identifying the Potentially Most Effective Strategies

Next you want to identify change strategies that will further the accomplishment of the organization's mission in ways that will solve a specific and recognized problem. The strategy should fulfill a unique niche—that is, either your organization is the only service provider in this area or you provide this service in a unique way unavailable from other organizations. It should help solve a problem that the organization is experiencing en route to achieve its mission.

The strategy needs to be high leverage in that if you are successful in accomplishing the strategy, other related issues will also be addressed. This is often

**TUI Decides on a High
Leverage Strategy**

Talent Unlimited, Inc. (TUI) assists
nonprofit organizations in their city
to build capacity to fulfill their
respective missions. It does this
through providing training and consulting services to the nonprofits
there that request their services.
Their problem is that their current
market is limited and does not
enable them to have the broader
impact they want.

As this is a huge job, the strategic question is: what will they do
and what won't they do? What new
strategy would help fulfill the mission, be within their organizational
capacity, solve a perceived problem,
have a market, and be high leverage—thus enabling other aspects of
leadership to improve as they con-
centrated on the single strategy?

TUI considered several strategies such as providing one-on-one
consulting to key nonprofit leaders
in the field, providing consulting
services to various nonprofit organizations, developing a leader
training program for current nonprofit leaders, and developing an
academy for those who aspire to
become nonprofit leaders.

These strategies all help further
the mission; however, there is
insufficient capacity and market to
provide one-on-one consultation to
leaders and there are several other
organizations that provide training
to current and aspiring leaders,
although TUI's approach is original
and effective.

(continued)

called a logic model: the stepwise impact on other issues by the accomplishment of the problem which you are addressing.

The strategy must be feasible—there must be sufficient resources (money, people, and time) available to accomplish it within the planned time frame. The organization needs the internal capacity and a supportive external environment to succeed with the change strategy.

Finally, the strategy must be revisited after the leading change analysis has been done as described in this book. It must also be reassessed periodically for midcourse corrections. And it is also important that the strategy be revisited at its conclusion. Did it solve the original problem?

Distinguishing Strategy from Action

A further distinction to be made is between "strategy" and "action." The strategy is the larger umbrella of a set of more specific tasks or activities ("actions") that will be undertaken to achieve it. When thinking through the change strategy, it is important to think more broadly—what larger framework are we trying to address and how? What is included and what is excluded? Only then can you determine the several specific actions required. The actions must fully support the overall strategy. So, using the TUI example, the strategy is to pursue the expansion of its products and services to nonprofit organizations in other cities. Actions to be taken to get this done might include setting up a virtual learning network among partner cities and conduction conferences to showcase their programs among others. Of course, the actions, if successfully implemented, should result in the accomplishment of the overall strategy and should be thought of as pieces of the puzzle to form the whole.

Common Mistakes to Avoid

In addition to knowing the essential elements, it is equally useful to know what pitfalls may await. In this way you can avoid them when possible. Because you are just starting out, what you do at this step is the foundation for everything that follows. Catching potential mistakes at this juncture can save grief later on.

Mistake #1: Thinking That a Mission Is Developed by a Single Leader

Developing a mission is not an isolated activity done by a single person or a small group of people. In order to have buy-in from across the organization, the creation of a mission (and the subsequent review and revision of a mission) requires negotiation and genuine input from across the organization. A main leadership skill needed for the creation of a mission statement is active listening. And, if there are several departments involved, their respective missions have to support the overall organization mission and align with the missions of the other departments. These should not duplicate or compete; each department should find its unique contribution.

Mistake #2: Addressing Too Much in a Single Strategy; Inability to Say "No"

Many leaders are tempted to "pack" a given strategy with several other strategies. They want to get everything done. The trick here is to be selective and narrow the strategy to a single thought that furthers your mission and is a niche where you can have a competitive advantage or offer a unique program or service. Doing one thing often means not doing something else, because your

> **TUI Decides on a High Leverage Strategy (*continued*)**
>
> However, a high leverage, niche strategy would seem to be expanding its reach by selling its products and services to nonprofit organizations in other cities. This would expand the reach of their innovative approaches to training from a single city to several places across the country. This strategy furthers the mission and fits within current organization capacity especially since a good deal could take place virtually.
>
> This strategy is high leverage as it involves doing business with organizations and leaders from across the country and could lead to the development of many new services and clients. It is also a unique niche because there are few other organizations doing work of this kind. Therefore, the change strategy identified by TUI is "to pursue the expansion of its products and services to nonprofit organizations in other cities."

capacity and resources are limited. Leaders must decide what they will not do—and they frequently skip this step.

Mistake #3: Confusing Strategies with Actions

Often, leaders confuse strategies with actions—mostly by citing actions instead of strategies. Both specify something that will be done. But actions are easier to think of because they are more specific and concrete. The more difficult conceptual work is to think of the larger strategy, which causes you to determine the approach to addressing the problem and what won't be done. Many times people skip right to the actions, only to find that they accomplish the specific actions but haven't solved the problem—because the actions had no conceptual grounding and were only isolated activities that had little collective impact on the problem. For example, it would be an "action" for a university to develop a new faculty training program in active learning. The strategy that this action supports is "to increase the university's effectiveness in teaching its students to be critical thinkers." Other actions might be revising course content or creating new student assessments.

TOOL: STRATEGY/ACTION ALIGNER

The Strategy/Action Aligner tool contains a summary of the plan for your change strategy. It should help you develop strategies and actions. Note that you should revisit this document after you have thought through the subsequent seven steps in this book. It is hoped you will gain valuable information from the steps in the leading change process to inform your plan and give you the best chance of success.

STRATEGY/ACTION ALIGNER

Leader's Self-Reflection Questions

- *What strategy(ies) are the highest leverage?*

- *Am I sure we aren't setting only easy, accomplishable strategies instead of reaching for strategies that will make a difference? (That is appropriate for the first strategy to be easily accomplishable in a short time frame, but it should pave the way for the larger change. See Early Win Wonder in Step 5.)*

- *Can I identify why this strategy should lead to solving the problem and reaching benchmarks along the way?*

- *Do I believe strongly that this strategy has a good chance of solving the problem?*

- *Am I sure that "strategies" and "actions" are not confused?*

- *Does the plan allow for monitoring and midcourse corrections and the possibility that this is not the right strategy to achieve the goal or objective?*

- *Are there competing priorities that are likely to get in the way of achieving the highest leverage strategy(ies)?*

ORGANIZATION'S MISSION: _____

PROBLEM TO BE SOLVED: _____

STRATEGIES (How will the objective be achieved?)	ACTIONS TO ACCOMPLISH THE STRATEGY (What will specifically be done to achieve the strategy?)	WHO IS RESPONSIBLE AND WHAT KEY PARTNERS WILL BE ENGAGED (for each action)?	TIME LINE BY MONTH (for each action)	TANGIBLE EVIDENCE AND MEASURABLE RESULTS (for each action)
CHANGE STRATEGY 1:	Action 1 for change strategy 1			
_____	Action 2 for change strategy 1			
CHANGE STRATEGY 2:				
_____				
CHANGE STRATEGY 3:				
_____				
CHANGE STRATEGY 4:				
_____				
DELIVERABLES (FOR EXAMPLE, REPORTS, PUBLICATIONS) WITH DUE DATES:				

Copyright © by John Wiley and Sons, Inc.

TALES

Using the tactics in this chapter, leaders of the composite organizations have each identified a change strategy and main actions. The following is an analysis of the organizations' strategies that will be followed in each subsequent chapter.

IHHS Decides to Expand Its Services to Asia

A problem for IHHS is the geographical limitations of its current body of work, which is centered primarily in the United States, Latin America, and Central and Eastern Europe. In order to create a competitive advantage in program development and funding, it would like to expand its services to new regions of the world. This would expand its reach and impact, provide a more internationally informed perspective for its international education programs and diversify its funding sources. An analysis of the external environment has found a market and available funding for work in the education sector of several countries in Asia.

By successfully accomplishing the following two actions, IHHS hopes to accomplish this strategy: (1) undertake collaboration with the Ministry of Education in "Pacifica" (a fictional composite of several countries) to reform the teacher training systems in that country, and (2) develop and implement a graduate student exchange program for students from Asian countries to pursue master's degrees from universities in the United States.

TUI Wants to Expand the Use of Its Products and Services to Nonprofit Organizations in Other Cities

TUI believes that the organization has a unique and successful approach to training and consultation in the nonprofit sector that would be of great benefit to its current market and beyond. Its problem is the limitations imposed on its growth, both programmatically and geographically, by the restrictions of serving only the needs of its locality. Its change strategy therefore is to expand the number of cities in the state who use the services of TUI or partner with TUI to improve their own capacity. The two main actions it will take are: (1) to promote its current products to other cities, including the potential for local adaptation of those products, and (2) to begin a virtual learning network of similar organizations in their own and other cities to share effective practice and aid the improvement of their programs.

Changeville School District Focuses on Programs and Services for Highest-Needs Schools

Changeville School District's main issue is to increase student achievement, but it would not be sufficient to do this by further improving the performance of the highest achievers; the district also seeks to improve the achievement of the highest needs students. The three main actions are (1) to develop new curriculum in mathematics, (2) to train school leaders in how to improve instruction for students with highest needs, and (3) to develop and implement a districtwide program to lower the number of students who drop out of school.

Turnaround School Seeks to Involve School Community in Developing New Ways to Engage Students in Learning

Turnaround School also seeks to improve the achievement of its students. Its change strategy is to involve the entire school community in developing new ways of engaging students in learning. Its two main actions will be: (1) to empower a leadership team to share decision making with the principal, and (2) to develop a professional learning community throughout the school community to develop new lessons and share effective practice with everyone.

WHAT ELSE IS NEEDED?

Throughout the subsequent chapters we will see how leaders at the state, district, and school levels used the tactics and tools to bring about their desired changes.

Assessing Readiness—

Where You Are Isn't Necessarily Where They Are

As an outside consultant, I always use the Readiness Rubrics when determining if organizations are really ready to become engaged in any change initiative. If they don't determine the readiness, and go through the appropriate steps, they are setting themselves up for very possible failure.

—A nonprofit leader

We have learned the hard way that members' readiness is crucial to the success of the work.

—A state leader

TACTICS

Once the change strategy has been determined, the next step is to determine the readiness of all concerned to engage in the effort. This includes those who will be implementing the change, the organization, and the leader him- or herself.

You have to identify your starting point and go from there. You must start from where you are; not where you *think* you are or where you *wish* you were— but where the data say you are. The story is sometimes told of an out-of-town family en route to a reunion in Cedar Rapids, Iowa, who find themselves lost in endless miles of farmland. Finally they see a farmhouse in the distance and joyously drive toward the building to make inquiry of the farmer working in front. When they tell the farmer that they are trying to get to Cedar Rapids, and ask how to go, the farmer replies: *"If you're trying to go to Cedar Rapids, I sure wouldn't start from here!"*

Nevertheless—you must be clear about where you are starting from in order to develop the best path from that point on. The objective in assessing readiness is twofold: to determine whether there is enough foundation for this initiative to enable it to succeed, and to develop a plan of action to improve the readiness for this change if the readiness is not strong but you still want to go ahead. Readiness will likely improve as you and your team have success with the endeavor. The question is: strategically, do you go ahead with one strategy or another? The answer might depend on how ready everyone is to go forward currently or what steps can be taken to improve the readiness, or both.

Essential Elements

Assessing readiness before embarking on your change strategy will help you diagnose what is needed to move forward and plan how to do so. The following are the main ingredients to this step.

Assessing the Readiness of the Leader

You have to know your own readiness for the new work. This requires thinking through how willing you are to go beyond your comfort level in order to accommodate the readiness of those on your team. Perhaps you are ready for change, but those with whom you work are not. Perhaps you like to treat all people as colleagues and give everyone equal voice. But, when it comes to readiness—you must change to accommodate the readiness of your team. It is far easier for one person to change than for twenty-five people to do so. You must be prepared to adjust your style to increase the readiness of the group. This means that a low readiness group needs high structure, regardless of your preference to let the group decide matters for itself, for example.

Leaders often have a reluctance to label a group as "low readiness" because they are colleagues—and leaders want to think the best of everyone. Being low readiness is not a judgment on the worth of the group. It is a reality that needs to be considered when planning activities to gain their active and constructive participation in the change strategy. Are you ready to assess the group and design your method of working with them accordingly?

Assessing the Readiness of the Individuals Involved ("Participants")

Then you want to find out how ready are those who are affected—those who will participate in planning and implementing the change strategy. Do they have successful previous experience with similar change strategies? Do they have the skills and knowledge in the content area of the strategy? Are they enthusiastic about the strategy and willing to take risks and responsibility? Do they have shared meaning perspectives and culture when it comes to the strategy? In other words, do participants believe that the strategy will further a shared value (such as improving the performance of high-needs students)? Do participants speak the same language when it comes to the strategy? Not only the same words, but the same meaning?

For example, when a district and university have a strategy to "co-construct" a new program, what understanding do they each have about what that entails? Does "co-construction" mean that the university will develop a program and ask for the input of the district? Does it mean that the district will develop the program and ask for the input of the university? That each entity will add some bells and whistles to an existing program? Or does it mean that the current program will be scrapped and both entities will work together from scratch to develop something completely new? Most often we assume that everyone shares the same definition—until the strategy fails due to differences in understanding of what was supposed to happen.

Assessing Organizational Readiness (Culture)

All organizations have ways of operating that are defined by the values and norms that are expected of those who work there. The degree to which an organization is ready for a given change strategy often relies on the degree to which that strategy furthers (or at least doesn't thwart) its values. In addition, there are certain organizational values that are supportive of change, and having these values prominent in the culture is a head start for any initiative: organizational learning, risk taking, and a willingness to learn from mistakes.

And you must take special care to work within the bounds of the organizational culture and values and not upset them inadvertently. For example, the new administration of a large nonprofit organization with an annual budget in the hundreds of millions of dollars once tried to save $300 per year by eliminating cakes and office celebrations on employees' birthdays. The hue and cry that resulted was enormous and disrupted the workplace until the practice was restored. The financial impact was small, but the cultural disruption was large.

Rating Readiness High, Medium, or Low

Should you decide to go forward, you need to know if readiness is high, medium, or low. The Readiness Rubric should help you make this assessment. Bear in mind that low readiness in any category indicates "low readiness" overall. And most groups and organizations undergoing a change will likely be low readiness because previous experience is probably lacking.

It is especially important to identify low readiness because—as the old saying goes—"the least committed party controls any relationship." Such low readiness groups will need much more structure and guidance until they experience success and have more confidence in the change process and in themselves as they help carry it out.

Using the Readiness Rating to Design Your Methods

In practice, you will want to employ different strategies to correspond with the readiness of any given group. For example, low-readiness groups need high-structure strategies, largely initiated by the leader, such as: specific, clear outcomes (objectives) with time lines and evaluation criteria; templates for work plans and budgets; written meeting agendas including ground rules for participation; written recording of decisions reached at a meeting that are promptly

A State Assesses Readiness When Developing New Curriculum Standards

A state was attempting to develop new curriculum standards in all grade levels and subjects. To do this, the change leader brought together key players from districts, schools, teacher unions, universities, the business community, and the state education department. It was immediately clear to the leader that "there was no meeting of the minds among us on how to approach the work. People were not participating collaboratively as members of this group. It was clear that there was something missing. Nothing was accomplished. In fact, harm was done given that we got no result."

When the planning team debriefed the meeting using the Readiness Rubrics, it became obvious that the readiness level of participants was low. The leader commented:

We had never thought of that since everyone at the meeting was a senior official and skilled educator. Nevertheless, we did not have a common language, a common definition of the problem, a common approach—and we had never worked together before as a group. Once we realized that the readiness was low, we planned a much more effective approach to the second meeting.

(continued)

distributed; continuous review of progress and midcourse corrections through a defined structure, such as regularly scheduled meetings; and structured questioning to lead group conversation (never ask an open-ended question to a low-readiness group).

Medium-readiness groups need moderate structure strategies such as: meeting agendas and ground rules jointly set between participants and the leader; shared responsibility for recording the decisions from meetings; and collaborative planning.

High-readiness groups should be self-directed in that they and the leader agree on the outcome or product needed and the group decides how to achieve it. The leader supplies resources identified by the group and is available for consultation.

Considering Individual Readiness as Well as Group Readiness

Because any group will include people with different levels of readiness, you should design strategies for participants of lowest readiness to reduce their chances of disrupting or slowing the change process. One technique for managing varying levels of readiness within the larger groups is to form smaller working groups according to participants' readiness and to structure the assignments of those working groups according to their readiness level.

Common Mistakes to Avoid

Knowing what not to do can be even more important than knowing what to do. Here are some pitfalls to avoid.

Mistake #1: Not Doing a Readiness Assessment

Of course, the most common mistake is not to do a readiness assessment. Sometimes this can be an oversight, but sometimes it can also be considered but rejected as unnecessary. As one state-level official nonprofit leader put it, "A mistake we made was to assume readiness because our participants were high level officials." She added, "We assumed readiness because we [the leaders of the organization] believed the topic to be crucial, and assumed they did as well. That turned out not to be the case."

Mistake #2: Not Testing Assumptions

We can now see the importance of assessing readiness at the beginning of the implementation of a change strategy and designing the work accordingly. However, that assessment has to be done thoroughly and honestly or the strategy will not be successful. Again, up for consideration is not "how ready do we think we are" or "how ready would we like to be" but "how ready are we... *really*?" TUI's tale at the end of this chapter illustrates this point well.

> **A State Assesses Readiness When Developing New Curriculum Standards (*continued*)**
>
> *We distributed a specific statement of the goal of the project, a charter of how the group would work together, and set up working groups for each subject area.*
>
> The second meeting was more successful, with all members following the procedures and thereby engaging in productive dialogue. There was agreement on what the work needed to be, how it would get done, what the results would be and when they would be ready. The districts, schools, and other partners will also be in a position to identify additional change strategies they need to design and implement in order to operationalize the curriculum standards. By then, they should be a high readiness group and ready for that task.

Mistake #3: Not Revisiting the Readiness for Every New Action

It is important to realize that levels of readiness will differ by task, even for the same group of participants. You will need to reassess readiness for each activity. If no information is available, assume low readiness. You can always lessen the structure later if you determine otherwise as you go along; better to begin with a lot of structure and lessen it later than to have to impose structure at a later point when it has been absent from the beginning.

Readiness levels are likely to improve as the group becomes successful, gains more skills, and develops more positive attitudes toward the change process. It is important to adjust your change strategies to take full advantage of increased readiness as it develops. If you don't recognize this difference, the group will "turn off" at being given less discretion than they have earned.

TOOL: READINESS RUBRICS

The Readiness Rubrics present specific questions that do not leave to chance whether you will fully consider all key aspects of readiness in your analysis. To make sure you do not make those common mistakes, Readiness Rubrics give you specific questions to think through. You should base your ratings on evidence.

The Readiness Rubrics can be used by the leader to rate the group's readiness from your own knowledge of the participants. Alternatively, you can ask participants themselves to assess their own readiness for the task. The data from the tool enables you to decide how much structure you will put into group activities. It also enables you to identify the area(s) on which to place greatest emphasis when trying to increase the readiness levels of the group. For example, gaining more successful experience can be attained through early wins (see the Early Win Wonder tool in Step 5), attitudes may be improved through use of the Resistance Reducer tool (Step 4), and skills/knowledge may be improved through training.

You will also want to use this tool to consider your own personal readiness for the change at hand and understand what you need to do to increase your readiness to accomplish the change strategy. There is a separate rubric for this purpose. You will find a completed sample Readiness Rubric in the Appendix.

READINESS RUBRIC

Change Strategy Under Consideration: _____

_____

_____

Note that many of the forms in this book can be downloaded for free from the Jossey-Bass Web site. Go to: www.josseybass.com/go/spiro.

SECTION A: LEADER'S READINESS

Readiness = Experience + Skills + Willingness + Shared Values

Be candid when completing this tool and try to think of concrete examples when answering the questions. Be careful when noting your ratings; the scale descriptions are not the same for all questions.

	RATING/SCORE

A. Experience: To what degree do you have previous experience with change in general and with this type of change in particular?

Answer the questions below by highlighting your score on the 5-point scale on the right.

Question	Rating/Score
1. Have you successfully led change in any organization before, especially an organization similar to the current one?	Many times Once or twice Never 5 4 3 2 1
2. Have you successfully led change in this organization before?	Many times Once or twice Never 5 4 3 2 1
3. Have you led change in any organization *unsuccessfully*?	Many times Once or twice Never 5 4 3 2 1
4. Do you have previous successful experience in the technical content area of the change strategy (i.e., management consulting, curriculum development, teaching science)?	A great deal Some None 5 4 3 2 1
5. Have you been able to "unfreeze" participants' previously negative experiences with change and motivate them to take a leap of faith now?	Always Sometimes Never 5 4 3 2 1
Experience Subtotal: Add your points scored for questions A1–A5. The total point score for "experience" is _____ out of 25 possible points. *Therefore, my readiness level regarding experience is (highlight one): HIGH, MEDIUM, LOW*	High readiness = 22–25 points Medium readiness = 15–21 points Low readiness = 14 points and below

Copyright © 2011 by John Wiley & Sons, Inc.

A. Required Skills: To what degree do you have the required skills and knowledge for this change strategy?

Answer the questions below by highlighting your score on the 5-point scale on the right.

		RATING/SCORE			
6. Do you have expertise in the content required by this change strategy? If not, do you have confidence in the expertise of others on your team?	A great deal 5	4	Mostly 3	2	Not as much as desirable 1
7. Are you skillful at leading change?	Very skillful 5	4	Somewhat skillful 3	2	Not at all 1
8. Are you aware of what you do not know and are you candid about it?	Always 5	4	Somewhat 3	2	Seldom 1
9. Are you willing to learn together with the participants when the skills and knowledge are just emerging?	Always 5	4	Somewhat 3	2	Seldom 1
10. Are you an active listener (i.e., para-phrasing, waiting 9 seconds for response after asking a question)?	Always 5	4	Somewhat 3	2	Seldom 1
Required Skills Subtotal: Add your points scored for questions A6–A10. The total point score for "experience" is _____ out of 25 possible points. *Therefore, my readiness level regarding skills is (highlight one): HIGH, MEDIUM, LOW*	High readiness = 22–25 points		Medium readiness = 15–21 points		Low readiness = 14 points and below

A. "Whatever it takes": To what degree are you willing to do whatever it takes?

Answer the questions below by highlighting your score on the 5-point scale on the right.

11. Do you have competing priorities that might demand your attention and detract from your leadership of the change strategy?	None 5	4	One or two 3	2	Several 1
12. Are you reluctant to label a group as "low readiness"? Are you reluctant to put a lot of structure into your planning and implementation processes?	Never 5	4	Sometimes 3	2	Always 1
13. Do you believe that you should always treat everyone equally as colleagues regardless of their readiness to partici-pate in the change strategy?	No 5	4	Somewhat 3	2	Yes 1

Copyright © 2011 by John Wiley & Sons, Inc.

Copyright © 2011 by John Wiley & Sons, Inc.

	RATING/SCORE				
14. Do you consult people whose views may differ from your own?	Always		Somewhat		Seldom
	5	4	3	2	1
15. Are you open to the resulting plan being different from your original conception (provided that the nonnegotiables are in there)?	Always		Somewhat		Seldom
	5	4	3	2	1
"Whatever it takes" Subtotal: Add your points scored for questions A11–A15. The total point score for "whatever it takes" is _____ out of 25 possible points. *Therefore, my readiness level regarding "whatever it takes" is (highlight one): HIGH, MEDIUM, LOW*	High readiness = 22–25 points		Medium readiness 15–21 points		Low readiness = 14 points and below

A. Values: To what degree do you have values that will propel the change process?

Answer the questions below by highlighting your score on the 5-point scale on the right.

16. Do you and the participants have the same definitions/language for the problem to be solved and the methods by which this will be undertaken? Has this assumption been tested?	Definitely		Perhaps		No or don't know
	5	4	3	2	1
17. Are you comfortable with taking risks and learning from mistakes?	Always		Somewhat		No
	5	4	3	2	1
18. Do you know the values of participants and of the organization and how they may differ from your own?	To a great extent		Somewhat		Not at all
	5	4	3	2	1
19. Do you value flexibility?	Always		Somewhat		Seldom
	5	4	3	2	1
20. Do you model behavior that you want to see as norms, such as adhering to ground rules?	Always		Somewhat		Seldom
	5	4	3	2	1
Values Subtotal: Add your points scored for questions A16–A20. The total point score for "values" is _____ out of 25 possible points. *Therefore, my readiness level regarding values is (highlight one): HIGH, MEDIUM, LOW*	High readiness= 22–25 points		Medium readiness = 15–21 points		Low readiness = 14 points and below

Section A Summary: Leader's Total Readiness Score (out of 100)

Sub-score for experience:	_____ out of 25	Readiness level: _____
Sub-score for skills:	_____ out of 25	Readiness level: _____
Sub-score for do what it takes	_____ out of 25	Readiness level: _____
Sub-score for values:	_____ out of 25	Readiness level: _____
TOTAL READINESS SCORE:	_____ out of 100	

LEADER'S READINESS LEVEL (highlight one): HIGH, MEDIUM, LOW

High = 88–100; Medium = 87–60; Low = below 60

Copyright © 2011 by John Wiley & Sons, Inc.

SECTION B: PARTICIPANTS' READINESS

Readiness = Experience + Skills + Willingness + Shared Values

Be candid when completing this tool and try to think of concrete examples when answering the questions. Be careful when noting your ratings; the scale is not the same for all questions.

	RATING/SCORE

B. Experience: To what degree do participants have previous experience with change in general and with this type of change in particular?

Answer the questions below by highlighting your score on the 5-point scale on the right.

	All have		Some have		Few have
1. Have participants successfully undergone change in any organization before?	5	4	3	2	1
2. Have participants successfully undergone change in *this* organization before?	All have 5	4	Some have 3	2	Few have 1
3. Have participants experienced change in this organization *unsuccessfully*?	All have 5	4	Some have 3	2	Few have 1
4. Do participants have previous successful experience in the content area of the change strategy?	All have 5	4	Some have 3	2	Few have 1
5. If participants' experience has been negative, are they willing to take a leap of faith now?	Definitely 5	4	Perhaps 3	2	Few will 1

Experience Subtotal: Add your points scored for questions B1–B5. The total point score for "experience" is _____ out of 25 possible points. *Therefore, participants' readiness level regarding experience is (highlight one): HIGH, MEDIUM, LOW*	High readiness = 22–25 points	Medium readiness = 15–21 points	Low readiness = 14 points and below

B. Required Skills: To what degree do participants have the required skills and knowledge for this change strategy?

Answer the questions below by highlighting your score on the 5-point scale on the right.

	Consistently		Sometimes		Infrequently
6. Have participants demonstrated expertise in the content required by this change strategy?	5	4	3	2	1

Copyright © 2011 by John Wiley & Sons, Inc.

	RATING/SCORE				
7. Do participants have formal training in the technical content required by this change strategy?	A great deal 5	4	Some 3	2	Little 1
8. Are training, research, and/or other resources available in the content required by this change strategy and will participants use them?	A great deal 5	4	Some 3	2	Little 1
9. Are participants aware of what they do not know and are they candid about it?	Completely 5	4	Somewhat 3	2	No 1
10. Are participants willing to learn together when the skills/knowledge are just emerging?	Eagerly 5	4	Somewhat 3	2	Seldom 1
Required Skills Subtotal: Add your points scored for questions B6–B10. The total point score for "skills" is _____ out of 25 possible points. *Therefore, participants' readiness level regarding experience is (highlight one): HIGH, MEDIUM, LOW*	High readiness = 22–25 points		Medium readiness = 15–21 points		Low readiness = 14 points and below

B. "Whatever it takes": To what degree are participants willing to do whatever it takes?

Answer the questions below by highlighting your score on the 5-point scale on the right.

11. Are participants passionate about solving this problem and enthusiastic about making it happen?	Definitely 5	4	Mostly 3	2	Not really 1
12. Are there many volunteers for various work assignments?	Always 5	4	Sometimes 3	2	Seldom 1
13. Do participants feel blamed for the problem's existence and complain they are being asked to change?	Not at all 5	4	Perhaps 3	2	Yes 1
14. Are participants not implementing well even though they have the skills and knowledge to do so?	No (implementation is on course) 5	4	Sometimes this is an issue 3	2	Frequently 1

Copyright © 2011 by John Wiley & Sons, Inc.

	Always		Sometimes but not the norm	Seldom (or only one or two reliable people)
15. Do most people come in early and/or stay until the job is done even if it is past the end of their official day?	**5**	**4**	**3**	**2** 1
"Whatever it takes" Subtotal: Add your points scored for questions B11–B15. The total point score for "doing whatever it takes" is _____ out of 25 possible points. *Therefore, participants' readiness level regarding doing whatever it takes is (highlight one): HIGH, MEDIUM, LOW*	High readiness = 22–25 points		Medium readiness 15–21 points	Low readiness = 14 points and below

B. Values: To what degree do participants have shared understandings (culture)?

Answer the questions below by highlighting your score on the 5-point scale on the right.

	Always		Sometimes		No or untested
16. Do participants have the same definitions/language for the problem to be solved and the methods by which this will be undertaken? Has this assumption been tested?	5	4	3	2	1
17. Are participants comfortable with taking risks and learning from mistakes?	Always 5	4	Somewhat 3	2	Seldom 1
18. Do participants value listening to each other, hearing what each is saying, and testing those assumptions?	Always 5	4	Somewhat 3	2	Seldom 1
19. Are participants comfortable with ambiguity?	Always 5	4	Somewhat 3	2	Seldom 1
20. Do participants value flexibility?	Always 5	4	Somewhat 3	2	Seldom 1
Values Subtotal: Add your points scored for questions B16–B20. The total point score for "shared understandings" is _____ out of 25 possible points. *Therefore, participants' readiness level regarding shared understandings is (highlight one): HIGH, MEDIUM, LOW*	High readiness= 22–25 points		Medium readiness = 15–21 points		Low readiness = 14 points and below

Copyright © 2011 by John Wiley & Sons, Inc.

Section B Summary: Participants' Total Readiness Scores

Sub-score for experience:	_____ out of 25	Readiness level: _____
Sub-score for skills:	_____ out of 25	Readiness level: _____
Sub-score for do what it takes	_____ out of 25	Readiness level: _____
Sub-score for values:	_____ out of 25	Readiness level: _____
TOTAL READINESS SCORE:	_____ out of 100	

LEADER'S READINESS LEVEL (highlight one): HIGH, MEDIUM, LOW

High = 88–100; Medium = 87–60; Low = 59 and below

Copyright © 2011 by John Wiley & Sons, Inc.

SECTION C: THE ORGANIZATION'S READINESS

Readiness = Organizational Experience + Organizational Learning + Organizational Culture + Shared Values About This Change Strategy

Be candid when completing this tool and try to think of concrete examples when answering the questions. Be careful when noting your ratings; the scale is not the same for all questions.

RATING/SCORE

C. Experience: To what degree does the organization have previous experience with change in general and with this type of change in particular?

Answer the questions below by highlighting your score on the 5-point scale on the right.

	Rating/Score
1. Has the organization successfully undergone any type of change before?	**Many times** **Once or twice** **Never** 5 4 3 2 1
2. Has the organization successfully undergone change in the same content area as the proposed change strategy before?	**Many times** **Once or twice** **Never** 5 4 3 2 1
3. Has the organization experienced change in this organization *unsuccessfully*?	**Never** **Once** **More than once** 5 4 3 2 1
4. Does the organization have experience in delivering programs similar in content to those of the change strategy?	**Has all needed expertise** **Has most needed expertise** **Has little needed expertise currently** 5 4 3 2 1
5. If the organization's experience has been negative, does it value risk-taking?	**A great deal** **To a moderate degree** **Seldom** 5 4 3 2 1
Experience Subtotal: Add your points scored for questions C1–C5. The total point score for "experience" is _____ out of 25 possible points. *Therefore, participants' readiness level regarding experience is (highlight one): HIGH, MEDIUM, LOW*	High readiness = 22–25 points Medium readiness = 15–21 points Low readiness = 14 points and below

Copyright © 2011 by John Wiley & Sons, Inc.

	RATING/SCORE

C. Organizational Learning: To what degree does the organization have the capacity to learn the skills that are required for this change strategy?

Answer the questions below by highlighting your score on the 5-point scale on the right.

6. Are there processes in place by which organization members critically reflect on their experiences with their programs (successful and unsuccessful)? If not, will such be put in place for this initiative?	**Definitely**		**Somewhat**		**Not at this time**
	5	4	3	2	1
7. Are there many types of learning taking place (i.e., formal training, informal learning)?	**On-going**		**Some**		**Little or none**
	5	4	3	2	1
8. Are research, data, and/or other resources available in the content area? Are they valued, used, and discussed?	**Extensive**		**Some**		**Little or none**
	5	4	3	2	1
9. Is there on-going assessment of each individual's skills versus those needed for his/her role – and a plan for developing skills that need improvement?	**A formal system is in place**		**Something is done; it might not be formal**	**Little or nothing is done**	
	5	4	3	2	1
10. Is there a vehicle for learning together when the skills and knowledge are just emerging?	**A formal system is in place**		**Something is done; it might not be formal**	**Little or nothing is done**	
	5	4	3	2	1

Organizational Learning Subtotal: Add your points scored for questions C6–C10. The total point score for "skills" is _____ out of 25 possible points. *Therefore, participants' readiness level regarding experience is (highlight one): HIGH, MEDIUM, LOW*	High readiness = 22–25 points	Medium readiness = 15–21 points	Low readiness = 14 points and below

C. Organizational Culture:

Answer the questions below by highlighting your score on the 5-point scale on the right.

11. Is there a culture of trying to assign blame when things go wrong or a value for being reflective and learning from mistakes?	**No or seldom**		**To some extent**		**Yes**
	5	4	3	2	1
12. Is there a shared value for flexibility? Ambiguity seen as opportunity?	**Always**		**Sometimes**		**Seldom**
	5	4	3	2	1

Copyright © 2011 by John Wiley & Sons, Inc.

Copyright © 2011 by John Wiley & Sons, Inc.

	RATING/SCORE		
13. Is there a culture of mutual respect? Is listening to each other valued?	Always 5 4	Sometimes 3 2	Seldom 1
14. Is there a strong organizational work ethic?	Always 5 4	Sometimes 3 2	Seldom 1
15. Are there rituals or ceremonies to celebrate successes?	Always 5 4	Sometimes 3 2	Seldom 1
Organizational culture Subtotal: Add your points scored for questions C11–C15. The total point score for "organizational culture" is _____ out of 25 possible points. *Therefore, participants' readiness level regarding doing whatever it takes is (highlight one): HIGH, MEDIUM, LOW*	High readiness = 22–25 points	Medium readiness 15–21 points	Low readiness = 14 points and below

C. Shared Values: Shared values about the change strategy?

Answer the questions below by highlighting your score on the 5-point scale on the right.

	RATING/SCORE		
16. Are the terms in use for the change strategy commonly understood? Has this assumption been tested?	Yes 5 4	Perhaps 3 2	No 1
17. Are there shared norms of behavior (such as ground rules and agendas for meetings as a matter of course)?	Yes 5 4	Somewhat 3 2	No 1
18. Is there a shared value for the importance of the problem being addressed by the change strategy?	Yes 5 4	Somewhat 3 2	No 1
19. Is there a shared belief that this change strategy will help solve the problem?	Yes 5 4	Somewhat 3 2	No 1
20. Is there a shared belief that this change strategy will be successfully implemented?	Yes 5 4	Somewhat 3 2	No 1
Shared Values Subtotal: Add your points scored for questions C16–C20. The total point score for "shared values" is _____ out of 25 possible points. *Therefore, participants' readiness level regarding shared understandings is (highlight one): HIGH, MEDIUM, LOW*	High readiness= 22–25 points	Medium readiness = 15–21 points	Low readiness = 14 points and below

Section C Summary: Organization's Total Readiness Score (out of 100)

Sub-score for experience:	_____ out of 25	Readiness level: _____
Sub-score for organizational learning:	_____ out of 25	Readiness level: _____
Sub-score for organizational culture:	_____ out of 25	Readiness level: _____
Sub-score for shared values:	_____ out of 25	Readiness level: _____
TOTAL READINESS SCORE:	_____ out of 100	

High = 88–100; Medium = 87–60; Low = 59 and below

TOTAL READINESS RECAP (TRANSCRIBE FROM YOUR TOTALS FROM SECTIONS A, B, AND C)

Leader's readiness level is (highlight one):	HIGH MEDIUM LOW
Participants' readiness is (highlight one):	HIGH MEDIUM LOW
Organization's readiness is (highlight one):	HIGH MEDIUM LOW

■ ■ ■

Determining Strategies to Accommodate and Improve Existing Readiness (of the Leader, the Participants, and the Organization)

- *What is the readiness of the leader? Of the participants? Of the organization?*

- *What are specific areas of high and low readiness for each? How will you accommodate them in your plans?*

- *Where are the gaps between participants and leader? Participants and organization? Leader and organization?*

- *What will you do to address those gaps?*

- *What type of structure will you build into your implementation plans? Which methods and how?*

Copyright © 2011 by John Wiley & Sons, Inc.

Strategies I Might Try as a Result of This Analysis

1. For the leader: _____

   _____

   _____

2. For the participants: _____

   _____

   _____

3. For the organization: _____

   _____

   _____

Copyright © 2011 by John Wiley & Sons, Inc.

Other Uses for the Readiness Assessment

We have seen that before beginning any change strategy, you will want to analyze the readiness of the participants, the organization, and the leader. Readiness assessments also come in handy when trying to select partners for the enterprise. For example, Changeville defined readiness criteria in its request for proposals for a university or nonprofit partner to work with them on developing leader training programs.

Another district uses the Readiness Rubrics as a device by which to have entry-level discussions with low-performing schools around how to improve instruction. The district had assigned a staff member to work with each low-performing school, but the staff was hesitant about beginning the discussions. They find that asking participants to complete the rubric and then having discussions about the results is a nonthreatening way to begin those discussions. They report that "the readiness rubric serves as an entry point to develop instructional teams and begin the discussions that accelerated the work."

TALES

Let's return to the tales from our four organizations and see how they assessed readiness for their change strategies and what effect that had.

IHHS Assesses Readiness When Selecting Its Team for Teacher Training Reform in Pacifica

Recall that one of IHHS's actions was to assist the country of Pacifica in redesigning the systems by which teacher training takes place throughout the country. The first question, therefore, was how to select a team of twelve capable experts in the training methods and content that would be required. IHHS defined the characteristics it sought in those who would lead the team and participate on it. The team leader had done such projects successfully in other countries in the region and had both content and training expertise. The organizational culture was well suited to this change strategy; it furthered its mission and values. All that was left was to recruit a high-readiness team.

So the selection process was announced with the criteria that matched those on the Readiness Rubrics (experience doing similar projects, expertise in the content areas, valuing education and collaboration in program development, and so on). The team of twelve enthusiastic and qualified professionals was assembled in a month and the team leader treated them as the high-readiness team they were. Unfortunately, once the team had to travel to Pacifica, the high readiness faded—as the experts became nervous and uncomfortable about their accommodations and whether security measures would be adequate. At this time, the team leader needed to reassess the readiness as low—and consequently built in much more structure, such as providing detailed travel itineraries including airport pick-up arrangements. That structure made the experts more comfortable, as they knew what to expect. In the case of IHHS, the leader knew to do a readiness assessment, and had to know to continue to reassess the readiness as the situation changed.

TUI Assesses—and Reassesses—Readiness to Participate in a Virtual Professional Learning Community

One action proposed to help achieve TUI's strategy of expanding its services to other cities was the creation of a professional learning community for non-profit leaders. As the organization began to think through how to implement this action, the first step was to assess the readiness of the leader, the participants, and the organization as a whole. What happened was quite interesting.

From all three perspectives, readiness was high and all seemed eager to begin. However, once they began the work, they discovered they were not so high readiness as they had thought. In fact, they and their clients were low readiness and thus needed to design their actions quite differently.

Both the leader and the employees at TUI were expert in planning and implementing large-scale, in-person conferences and therefore rated the implementers high on "previous experience" and "skills and knowledge." They also were enthused about this strategy. The organization culture strongly valued education and sharing of learning.

All these factors, they felt, pointed to high readiness for the strategy. The main pitfall of their analysis was that they did not know what they didn't know, which was conducting learning in a virtual space. As a result the strategy did not work at first and needed immediate course correction. TUI began the learning community with a large in-person conference, something indeed that they were expert in doing. It was very well received; everyone left the conference feeling positive about this endeavor.

However, weeks after the conference, the confidence faded as none of the follow-up assignments from participants were done and no further communications took place. In fact, nothing was happening at all. This was very discouraging. Where were the high-readiness leader and staff and the high readiness participants? Was this the wrong strategy after all? Was there really no interest? Should the strategy be discontinued?

Not at all. The change strategy could be effective with different tactics. The key would be to recognize that the leader, the implementers, the clients, and the organization were all low readiness, not high; therefore, they needed a great degree of structure in the actions, not the participant "self-direction" that was used.

The big difference between the analysis and reality was that conducting virtual learning was very different from in-person workshops and conferences. Although the leader and the implementers knew how to conduct in-person learning, they had never facilitated an online community. Nor had the participants ever successfully participated in one. Some had been part of such a community, but did not have a good experience.

The skills required to implement online were quite different from those possessed by the current staff. In addition, participants' previously unsuccessful experiences had to be "unfrozen" before they could participate fully. In terms of organization culture, although education was valued there was an implicit understanding that "education" was in-person and interpersonal. There was no similar value for technology. Therefore, no one was high readiness for this strategy. Yet, they were being treated as a high-readiness group, being asked to attend a conference and follow that with participation in subsequent project group work virtually.

Instead of scrapping the strategy, the leader undertook another readiness assessment and understood the low readiness of all concerned. Immediate action to put structures in place did the trick. Specific assignments were given to the project work groups and a facilitator was appointed to oversee the work. The facilitator was responsible for setting tasks and time lines and organizing group meetings—some virtual, some by conference call, and some in person. There was also a new deadline for all groups to have a specified, interim work product by the time of the next meeting—three months away.

The project work groups all got busy, and most of them met their deadline with a work product by the next face-to-face meeting. It was the structure that made the difference and the professional learning community strategy turned out to be a success. Again, although this experience happened with TUI, it is quite similar to what might happen when any organization tries to implement a new strategy.

Changeville Assesses Readiness for a New Leader Training Program

The district was mired in always trying to improve what *was* rather than aiming toward *what could be.* It was critical to engage partner organizations to create the new training program for leaders who thought in this new way. So the district assessed the readiness of potential partners for working in this type of approach by including questions in the *Request for Proposals* to which potential partners responded. Nonnegotiables delineated were "co-construction and co-delivery with the district, and use of problem-based scenarios from the real life experienced in the district." This would be an innovative approach. Was there a partner out there willing to work with the district in this new way? Indeed there was and the district selected an excellent partner organization.

The proposal submitted by the winning organization was on the cutting edge and created an impressive team of experts ready to work together. From there they assembled a strong team and had the first meeting. And then, a district leader tells this story:

> *I remember leaving the first meeting. I drove down the highway on a major interstate under the influence of confusion; disappointed; and wondering if these were the same people that were referenced in the proposal. It was as if the proposal writers had used the best thinking and research to obtain the award, but the implementing team did not hold the same core values and beliefs of the research in actuality. Unfortunately, it was business as usual.*

Only after that meeting did they realize that the problem was a low level of readiness in the group. Although they had attempted to recruit a high-readiness partner, once the larger group was put together (the district and the partner), together they were low readiness. They did not share common language about the meaning of "co-construction," for example, and needed to be brought to the same page on how to approach the task at hand. Therefore, there had to be a much more structured approach to the development processes. They had to identify those who had done this type of co-construction to guide the process because they had traveled this road and could predict where the barriers would be. They had to be agenda-led and time bound.

They began to use guidelines, agendas, and protocols to guide conversations and decision making. And it worked. The leader comments further:

> *The curriculum was developed, delivered, and assessed after that first year. Now in the third year of this work, we continue to assess our readiness. We continue to review our norms of behavior. We continue to create collaborative planning with individuals from diverse backgrounds and experiences so that the product gets better. We continue to grapple with ideas and theories until we get "there" wherever "there" happens to be. We continue to see this as a circular loop, rather than linear.*

Turnaround School Assesses Readiness for Developing New Lesson Plans

This high-readiness school has a leadership team where all members had developed curricula in their subject areas in the past and were eager to try out new curriculum approaches. The school values trying out new things, evaluating how it works, and making revisions. The faculty voted in favor of participating in the curriculum development and piloting.

Volunteer administrators, teachers, and students agreed to develop lesson plans and courses of study in accordance with the new state curriculum standards and bring the results to the leadership team on a biweekly basis for critical analysis. The technology teacher agreed to set up a Web site by which these lesson plans could be shared in an ongoing way with the school community. This self-directed approach worked well in this high-readiness school. Had a standard curriculum been imposed, surely the school community would have been highly resentful.

⬤ WHAT ELSE IS NEEDED?

Be aware that not all issues come up in readiness assessments. Once you know how ready the participants, organization, and the leader may be, there are other issues that arise—namely politics. Once you know everyone's readiness levels, there is another analysis that must be done to "start from where you are." You need to know where you are politically.

Analyzing the Stakeholders—

Who Cares? Why? and What Can They Do About It?

When I became a principal, I thought I would be leading instruction. I had no idea that the job would be so much about managing politics. Once I figured that out, I began to get things done.

—A high school principal

TACTICS

For the leader of change, one of the most important misconceptions is that it is enough to have a good idea that you believe will benefit the work. By definition, if things are to change in a significant way, stakeholders will often see themselves as winners or losers—even after the benefits become apparent. Regardless of how good a change strategy is, there are groups that are benefiting from the status quo and therefore may feel threatened, angry, or disempowered if things change.

Therefore, leading change effectively means accomplishing your goals in spite of opposition. So it is important for leaders to recognize which groups might lose power or influence with the proposed changes, minimize their opposition, provide openings for them to participate in devising improvements to the change strategy—but also to plan for opposition that cannot be addressed. This is all another way to say that you must address the politics inherent in leading any change strategy.

Essential Elements

When thinking through how to proceed, your actions should be tailored to engaging the various stakeholder groups whose support you will need. This includes analyzing not only which groups will be most influential, but also which facets of the change strategy are more or less political. There are several keys to engaging stakeholders.

Identify Winners and Losers and What They Stand to Gain and Lose

You will need to survey the landscape to identify who stands to gain or lose from the contemplated change. Of those groups, you need to understand which have the power to derail the change you are seeking. Once you know which they are, you can try to minimize such opposition by providing incentives to entice potential opponents to support the change, and thereby determine mutual self-interest.

Engage the Opponents Who Have the Power to Derail the Change Strategy

Of course it is not important only to *identify* the groups that are likely to oppose you and have the power to derail the change effort, it is important to engage them actively in the planning and implementation. You want to do this for at least two reasons: one is that they likely will bring to the table new perspectives that will add value and second is that they may be persuaded to appreciate the value of the change strategy by being part of its development. In any case, you will know what is on their minds.

Identify and Use Incentives

Most groups will be willing to collaborate if they have incentives to do so. Incentives can come in many forms: resources (money, people, and time), training, access to decision makers, and especially having a voice in making policy. The leader of a university faculty union frequently complained to the administration and wrote letters to the board of trustees. He represented a powerful constituency, but was routinely ignored in his critiques.

However, once he was invited to participate in the planning of a major initiative, he quickly became one of the most constructive and productive champions for this change. He became a key leader and was instrumental in bringing about important change. All that was needed was to redirect his passion by giving him and his constituency the incentive of having a true voice in leading change.

Within Your Change Strategy, Identify the Urgent Problems

You can lessen the politics of any given situation by addressing a change strategy that most groups perceive as urgent. In such situations, groups are usually willing to put aside other issues in order to get the urgent job done. An example can be seen when policy dictates that a school will be closed or redesigned unless it meets certain standards of student achievement. In this case, most groups within the school and the community will be more willing to work together to achieve the required improvement. It is important to realize, however, that although urgency mitigates politics in the short-term, the politics will resume once the urgency has passed.

Within the Urgent Problems, Find Those Eliciting Relatively Less Interest or Passion

It is also useful to begin the change process by focusing on areas in which some stakeholder groups are less interested, for whatever reason. There will be less opposition in these cases. Less opposition should result in early success which results in credibility and momentum. Then you are in a better position to tackle changes that will encounter greater opposition.

However, you must always test your assumptions. If you *think* your change strategy will engender relatively less interest of passion, make sure you test that out first.

For example, a few years ago a large city decided to dispense with the fire alarm boxes that were on many street corners. In the age of cell phones, it was determined that these relics were anachronistic and would not be missed. When officials removed the first fire alarm boxes, they were greatly surprised at the hue and cry that arose on this issue. Some citizen groups were up in arms at what they perceived to be a serious safety issue for their communities. The administration had to reconsider its policy, given the public outcry.

A State's Lessons About Assessing Stakeholders

A state wanted to revamp how education leaders were certified and trained. New laws were needed. Therefore, a wide variety of stakeholder groups were brought together to develop legislation. They included the governor's office, legislators, the state board of education, the state department of education, the Business Roundtable, and other statewide organizations (such as school districts, public and private universities, unions and professional associations). Fifteen groups were involved.

Since the consortium was open to any interested groups in the state, membership fluctuated and new members were always joining. This required constantly analyzing the stakeholders. It required analyzing how each group could participate in the legislation's success or failure both before and during the legislative process. The gains and losses for the main stakeholder groups were analyzed as follows:

- *For the State Board of Education*

  Gains: Increased role in developing and supporting new and experienced principals in the state

  Losses: Despite decreased staffing, increased responsibility and duties for improved leadership training in the state without funding for agency staff

- *For Administrator Organizations*

  Gains: Opportunity to take the lead in providing leadership training and support to principals in the state; state funding to run leadership training (e.g., new principal mentoring) and professional development for schools; increased visibility to recruit more members

  Losses: Opposition from members who are not comfortable with new set of expectations; increased competition from other organizations in the state vying for management of new state programs

  (continued)

- **For Regional Offices of Education**

  Gains: *Opportunity to increase services to schools by offering new leadership training and support; state and district funding to run leadership training and professional development*

  Losses: *Threat of other organizations acquiring these services so that districts and schools might start to look to them and not the regional office of education as the venue*

- **For Teacher Unions**

  Gains: *Opportunities for teachers to gain leadership experience and knowledge through a teacher leadership endorsement; provides higher-quality leadership to support the work of teachers*

  Losses: *Principals might be spending more time out of the building attending training programs*

- **For Urban School Districts**

  Gains: *State-funded support to improve the quality of leadership in the district; improvements in professional development offerings to principals as well as opening up the channel for the district to get approval to offer their own professional development*

  Losses: *Fear of new state requirements watering down the district's current rigorous requirements for principal evaluation and support; difference in philosophy between state and district vision for teacher leadership endorsement; loss of local control of principal training and support*

- **For Suburban and Rural School Districts**

  Gains: *Opportunity to improve quality of their leadership as supported by state funding; increased pool of potential leaders and leadership support through teacher leadership endorsement programs*

  Losses: *Accessibility to quality training limited by location in the state (especially for small rural districts)*

- **For Universities**

  Gains: *Opportunity to increase services to schools by offering new leadership training and support; state and district funding to run leadership training and professional development; opportunity to increase enrollment by offering new teacher leadership endorsement program*

  Losses: *Greater competition within other universities vying for the same services, programs, and student population*

What Happened and What Was Learned?

Through the stakeholder analysis it was determined that membership organizations (such as professional associations and unions) had the most credibility with the field so those became the stakeholders with the highest leverage. State leaders made sure that all stakeholders who stood to gain or lose from the change were involved with the process. To do this, staff used the stakeholder strategizer to identify supporters, opponents, areas of greatest urgency, and areas that excited relatively fewer passions. Making sure that everyone was at the table for this process ensured a better product and more stakeholder buy-in, which eased policy development and the implementation process.

As a result of this strategizing work, legislation progressed through both the House and the State Senate with unanimous support, something that rarely occurs with a piece of legislation this significant. However, there was one halt in the process, which occurred when one of the groups objected to the legislation at the last minute. They insisted on an amendment that seemed fairly minor. The work stopped.

The reason behind their show of power was that, although they were at the table for the conceptualization of the legislation and supported it, they were not represented in the actual writing of the bill. They, however, viewed their involvement in the actual writing as critical and therefore did not support a bill to which they had not written.

Therefore, one lesson learned through this process was that there are many times throughout the process when stakeholder analysis needs to happen: at the beginning with conceptualization and again during the actual writing of the legislation, where simple wording can change the whole intent. In hindsight, state leaders realized that they had underestimated that groups perceived that they gained power by being involved in the actual writing of the legislation—which is what upset the previous dynamic and called for a new stakeholder analysis.

After another year's work, the state legislature passed groundbreaking legislation that strengthened the state's system for licensing and supporting aspiring, new, and experienced principals. Reflecting back to the stakeholder analysis results for this phase of work would have helped them identify the brewing conflict and to integrate all groups into the work at this stage. Doing so would have saved much frustration. They did manage to set it right, but the conflict and bad feeling could have been avoided.

Common Mistakes to Avoid

Mistakes can be costly in terms of time and good will. It is difficult to recover from missteps. Here are some common mistakes that can be avoided once you are aware of them.

Mistake #1: Not Identifying Winners and Losers

The most common mistake is to not analyze the stakeholders at all and assume that everyone has a common agenda. When you are leading a change, you are likely to think the strategy is a good idea—why wouldn't everyone else also think so? You have learned why not in this chapter! There will always be groups that are benefiting from the way things are and will "lose" if your change strategy is implemented.

Mistake #2: Reluctance to Label a Group as Less Powerful and Needing Less Attention

In the same way that some leaders are reluctant to label a group as "low readiness," they are sometimes hesitant to take groups out of consideration if they have little power. Nevertheless, this is essential. You simply cannot accommodate the agendas of all groups; you must concentrate on those that have the power to push the change forward or derail it.

Mistake #3: Assuming That Groups Will Take Similar Positions on all Strategies

Few groups will consistently support or oppose you all the time. As with readiness, the analysis must be done on an issue-by-issue basis. A group that opposes you on today's strategy might well support you tomorrow. This is not personal; it is about getting agendas accomplished. Sometimes your agendas will be in sync and sometimes not. You need to know the difference.

As with the readiness assessment, analysis of stakeholders should not be thought of as a one-time occurrence. Stakeholders' positions change as the situation changes, so it is important to do the following analysis continuously throughout the change process.

Mistake #4: Not Knowing Exactly What You Want

If you don't know what you want from the stakeholders, you will get it only by accident. You have to know what is nonnegotiable for you and make that transparent. Then you will be able to negotiate any other aspect of the change strategy with the stakeholders in good faith.

Mistake #5: Getting Discouraged When You Encounter Opposition

Opposition is to be expected. Some group or groups are benefiting from the way things are and will oppose even the best idea for change—not on its merits, but because they will lose what they currently have. The tactics in this chapter should help you overcome this opposition, or at least understand from where it comes as you continue to pursue your change strategy.

TOOL: STAKEHOLDER STRATEGIZER

The Stakeholder Strategizer tool is most effectively used as a brainstorming device where several members of the planning team consider what they know about the various groups that will be involved in the change process. Knowing which groups may support or oppose you and why—and assessing their ability to promote or derail the change—will enable you to develop strategies to engage those groups that you identify as having the power to stall your efforts.

Understanding which strategies are less controversial can also lead to tackling that issue first and, once having had success, going on to more challenging aspects of your change strategy. And publicizing your early success will help build support for further successes along the way.

Using the data from this tool will also enable the leader to negotiate "at the margins"—that is, finding ways to accommodate at least some of the concerns of key groups without compromising the essence of the change strategy. The analysis provided by the tool also enables the leader to use data to make decisions purposefully about how to engage specific groups and to build on what each key group will perceive as a sense of urgency for the change initiative.

STAKEHOLDER STRATEGIZER

It is important to take the time to identify the political positions of the groups involved in the change process—as well as your own. The Stakeholder Strategizer tool takes you through these important reflections.

Leader's Self-Reflection Questions

- *Are all the right groups under consideration?*
- *Am I prepared to identify some groups as more important politically than others and address the engagement effort to them?*
- *Have I identified all the nonnegotiable actions of the change strategy and made them transparent?*
- *Am I willing to bargain about all other actions?*
- *Am I reluctant to label something "of less interest" because that might mean that something I consider important is not perceived that way?*

I. Which groups have power/influence over larger constituencies?

  A. What groups can help the proposed change succeed (supporters)?

GROUP	HOW?
1.	1.
2.	2.
3.	3.
4.	4.

■　■　●

Copyright © by John Wiley and Sons, Inc.

B. What groups can thwart the proposed change (opponents)?

GROUP	HOW?
1.	1.
2.	2.
3.	3.
4.	4.

■　■　●

II. What do supporters and opponents stand to gain or lose from the change strategy?

	GROUP	GAINS	LOSSES
SUPPORTERS (in order of importance)	1.	1.	1.
	2.	2.	2.
	3.	3.	3.
	4.	4.	4.
OPPONENTS (in order of importance)	1.	1.	1.
	2.	2.	2.
	3.	3.	3.
	4.	4.	4.

Copyright © by John Wiley and Sons, Inc.

· · ·

III. Therefore, groups that can help the proposed change, but are likely to lose something are:

_____

_____

_____

· · ·

IV. Groups that can thwart the proposed change and are likely to lose something are:

_____

_____

_____

V. What would each key group consider to be urgent regarding the change strategy?

	GROUP	WHAT WOULD THEY CONSIDER URGENT? HOW CAN THAT URGENCY BE ADDRESSED IN THE CHANGE STRATEGY?
1.		
2.		
3.		
4.		

Copyright © by John Wiley and Sons, Inc.

VI. What incentives can be given to the opponents to engage them?

GROUP (IN ORDER OF IMPORTANCE)	INCENTIVE	WHY IT SHOULD WORK
1.	1.	1.
2.	2.	2.
3.	3.	3.
4.	4.	4.

VII. Where are the areas of relatively less interest and how can they be used?

POTENTIAL AREA OF LESS INTEREST	HOW TO USE
1.	1.
2.	2.
3.	3.

VIII. Therefore stakeholder strategies might include:

1. _____

_____

_____

Copyright © by John Wiley and Sons, Inc.

2. _____

_____

_____

3. _____

_____

_____

4. _____

_____

_____

5. _____

_____

_____

Determining Strategies to Engage Stakeholders

Once you have identified those influential groups that can help you or derail you—and what each group stands to gain or lose, you are in a position to plan their engagement in making the change strategy happen. You will be able to identify the incentives each group might respond to, what each group might consider to be urgent, and which parts of the change strategy might excite relatively fewer passions—and be easier to implement. As long as you have already identified what is nonnegotiable and made that explicit, this is your opportunity to develop approaches to:

- _Identify which groups should get your attention in negotiations (and which should not)_

- _Increase the wins for supporter groups that are in danger of losing something as a result of the change strategy_

- _Build on the wins for supporter groups that are going to win something_

- _Build on the anticipated wins or mitigate anticipated losses for opponents in an attempt to engage them_

- _Use areas of perceived urgency and fewer passions as first actions, because they are most likely to result in less politics and thus greater success_

Copyright © by John Wiley and Sons, Inc.

TALES

Let's check in with our four organizations as they pursue the change strategies identified in Step 2 by analyzing their stakeholders.

IHHS Analyzes the Stakeholders of the Teacher Training Reform in Pacifica

As the work began in Pacifica, there were five main stakeholders—and from three countries. There was a Dutch nonprofit that, although a partner in the project, resented not being the lead agency and had an agenda to prove that the project would fail under the leadership of IHHS.

There was the local Pacifica nonprofit partner that was supportive because the project added to that organization's prestige and influence. And there was the funding organization, which wanted to see the project succeed, and the Ministry of Education of Pacifica that was ambivalent because the success of the project might break its monopoly on teacher training. And, of course, IHHS was a stakeholder, since success with this project was important for the overall goal of expanding the organization's work into Asia.

The urgency of replacing the current system was felt keenly among all parties; thus, they were willing to put their own agendas aside. It would excite relatively fewer passions to begin by training a new cadre of professional trainers instead of trying to build new institutions or redesign those that had existed for hundreds of years. Starting there was the least risky approach for all five groups.

Of the five stakeholder organizations, three were supportive and stood to gain while two could have derailed the venture and perceived that they had something to lose. It was the Dutch organization and the Pacifica Ministry of Education that could derail the effort.

IHHS had two nonnegotiables: the project had to begin immediately and it had to succeed. The IHHS leader negotiated incentives with each stakeholder group: the Dutch organization could take a lead role in organizing the first activity; the local partner was highlighted in the local press as a key player in the work; the funder was pleased with the immediacy of the start-up; and the ministry was pleased that it delayed or possibly derailed any attempt to create competing teacher training organizations.

TUI Analyzes the Stakeholders in Its Potential Expansion to Other Cities

In the case of TUI's proposed expansion to other cities, the organization was high readiness and there were several influential stakeholder groups in support, including organizations in other cities, national associations of professionals in this field, and several funders. All these groups felt that there was much to gain as the excellent programs and services of TUI would be of value in other contexts.

The "only" opposing group was very powerful—the board of directors! The board felt that they had a lot to lose in that they feared that the services that TUI was providing in their own city would be diluted by directing their attention elsewhere.

Once the board's rationale for objecting was understood, it was possible to assuage those concerns by negotiation. There would be a separate organization set up to plan and implement the expansion. All the services in the current city would remain untouched as the new organization planned and oversaw the expansion. This approach secured the support of the board because, under these circumstances, expansion would not have a negative impact on the current level of service and would bring even greater recognition and credibility to the organization. Also attractive, and winning the day, was the argument that diversifying the market was a good strategy for sustainability.

The Changeville Board of Education Analyzes Stakeholders for Development of a Core Curriculum in Mathematics

Throughout the school district, data showed that children were performing poorly in mathematics. It was clear to everyone that the district had to develop new curricula and assessments in this subject. Therefore, the superintendent brought stakeholders together from across the district and used the Stakeholder Strategizer to identify supporters and potential opponents.

Supporters would be the school board members, district administrators, school leaders, parents, and teachers with three to ten years' experience. Opponents would be teachers with more than ten years' experience (who had their lessons set) and new teachers (who were already overwhelmed and didn't want to change one more thing).

Everyone saw the urgency. The data were clear that students were performing poorly in mathematics—particularly disadvantaged students in all schools. Data collected included state assessments, skills assessment, common assessments, and classroom assessments. Based on these data, no one disagreed with the urgency to make change. And this was an area of less passion in opposition—who could object to improving mathematics scores?

In order to get all stakeholders to buy in, they assembled all math teachers including opponents and resisters and involved them in the planning phase of lesson, unit, and assessment development for mathematics at each graduated level (primary, intermediate, middle school, and high school). When the committee was organized, the ideas flowed easily. For example, the group decided to share student achievement data among colleagues so that those who achieved improvements could share their methods with others.

Turnaround School Analyzes the Stakeholders for Developing New Lesson Plans in Mathematics

The principal of Turnaround School, similarly, used the Stakeholder Synthesizer when trying to develop new mathematics lessons. She reported, "This tool helped us see that, at each grade level, there was a group of supporters. Therefore we decided that we could hold productive grade-level meetings to develop lessons to improve mathematics instruction. We knew that key groups of teachers would support the effort. We asked the groups to keep data notebooks and refer to them at weekly planning meetings. This led to rich discussions and new instructional strategies."

■ WHAT ELSE IS NEEDED?

Now that you have identified the groups needed to participate in the change strategy, you should go back and make sure you have included them in your readiness assessment of "participants." If any groups are missing, this is the time to complete the participant Readiness Rubric for them and use the results in your planning as you go forward.

Now we see the importance of understanding how various groups will react to the change strategy and how to approach their involvement. However, groups are made up of people. A group may take a position that furthers its mission and agenda, but the individuals who work for that group each may have their own reactions and feelings about change in general and the specific change strategy in particular. The next step is to address those individual reactions that result most often in resistance.

Minimizing Resistance—
While Maximizing Your Tolerance for It

We know buy-in is important, but we tend to focus on the content of the program and not the processes. Analyzing resistance up front has proven to be invaluable. By using the Resistance Reducer, we were able to determine what we needed to do to get the change strategy accepted. If we had not done this we would have been reacting to what the resistors thought they heard instead of identifying what they could support.

—A state leader

TACTICS

Using the tools in the preceding chapters should give you a head start on preventing resistance—by assessing and improving participants' readiness and identifying potential opponents and either bringing them on board or minimizing their ability to derail your plans. There is a good chance that resistance can be prevented if the process is matched to the readiness of the participants, and strategies are in place to engage key stakeholder groups.

Nevertheless, resistance is likely to occur. All change is associated with transition and loss—even when the change is for the better and perceived as such. If things are going to be different, something will be lost by definition. Often the request for change is "heard" by those being asked to change as "blaming" ("If what I was doing was effective, why are you asking me to change?"). Some people are uncomfortable with the unknown and sometimes they are asked to change too many things simultaneously. Indeed there is much to take into account when analyzing potential resistance and what can be done to minimize it. And the leader has to determine how much resistance you are willing to tolerate to get this strategy accomplished.

It is important to realize that you may encounter resistance even from individuals who are members of groups you have determined to be supporters. That the *group* may support the change strategy is one thing; *individuals* who make up the group are likely to feel insecure, threatened, confused, or anxious. Resistance is not about getting agendas accomplished as it was with the stakeholder analysis. It is about the feelings of those who are being asked to participate. Indeed, they may (or may not) support the change initiative in concept, but individuals may feel threatened, insecure, uncertain, or blamed. You need to be able to recognize this reaction when it is occurring.

Types of Resistance

Resistance is sometimes easy to see and sometimes not. Although it can be unpleasant to encounter, the easiest type of resistance to identify comes when someone is outspoken with his or her objections. At least you know what you're up against. Less obvious is when someone is silent about objections. You may or may not know what is happening.

The most difficult kind of resistance, however, comes from someone who appears to agree in public, but resists in action; the person who says one thing and does another. You have to be on the lookout for such behavior and not, as is common, accept the spoken words of agreement because that is what you would prefer to hear. Actions speak louder than words.

Essential Elements

As the leader, you must always ensure that the following elements are contained in your approach to leading the change initiative. You need to make sure that there are more advantages than disadvantages as perceived by the participants that your messages communicate what they will hear as opposed to what you think you are saying, and that your actions that advance existing organizational values or at least do not take away from them. In addition, you must assess your own tolerance for resistance so you can develop tactics to minimize resistance and know to what point the resistance will be a deal-breaker for you.

More Advantages Than Disadvantages as Perceived by Those Affected

Remember that change is a highly personal experience; each individual affected must come to believe that there are more benefits than costs if the change succeeds. You need to identify as many barriers to success as you can and eliminate them. Therefore, the first perspective to consider is what affected individuals will perceive as benefits and barriers to the change strategy. Doing so is the first step toward developing action steps that will emphasize the pluses and minimize the negatives. Most people will embrace change if its value is proven to them. "Enlightened self-interest" is natural and needs to be taken into account. The change strategy with

---

What Is Heard Is in the Ear of the Listener—Part One

A group of twenty-two rural schools were planning how they might work together to continue to offer excellent services to their students in the current economic downturn. They explored the following strategies: regionalization, virtual campuses, and sharing programs and staff.

When they brought these ideas back to their local communities it soon became clear that people heard the ideas in the following ways: regionalization equaled consolidation. Virtual campuses meant "there goes my kid's chance to star on the football team." Sharing programs and staff meant my school's personnel will be held harmless. It is the personnel at the "sharing" school that will be affected.

Unless the message was transparent and clear to all those affected, there would be significant resistance to any of these strategies as they proceeded.

the highest likelihood of success is where there is something important in it for everyone…even if that "something important" is different for each person.

Messages Communicated Through the Participants' Ears Not Your Own

The second perspective is reflecting on listening skills—what your audience actually hears when you talk. That is, you can take steps to minimize resistance by thinking like the intended audience. *You* may fully understand what you are trying to communicate, but the *audience* may be misunderstanding, or hearing something different from what you intended. A successful change leader therefore probes, listens actively, and paraphrases.

In fact, a really effective leader waits a full nine seconds for response after asking a question. That's a long time and few leaders really wait that long. But by doing so you will get thoughtful and insightful comments that you would likely miss otherwise.

To really understand the barrier to successful communications through participants' ears, it is useful to picture a political candidate trying to get his message across to a focus group. If you could see the thought bubbles above each individual's head as he was talking, you would "see" each individual's thoughts such as: "How does this further *my* agenda?" and "What does this mean for *me*?" No one is really hearing what the candidate is saying, but he thinks he is getting his message across. Group members are filtering his message through their own hopes and concerns.

Organizational Culture Is Furthered by the Change Initiative

Because any change is stressful, it is important that—if your change strategy does not involve changing organizational values—you use the furthering of existing organizational values to help those affected feel comfortable with the new changes. Organizational culture can be a web of comfort for most people, providing routines and therefore comfort and stability.

> ### What Is Heard Is in the Ear of the Listener—Part Two
>
> An elementary school principal wanted to ask the school community for their advice in helping her become an instructional leader. She first consulted the leadership team which wrote down key phrases and assessed her in determining what individuals might hear when she asked for this assistance. For example, when the principal says she wants to be an instructional leader, people might hear "Aren't you that already?" When she says that she wants to be in classrooms more often, teachers hear "Don't you trust me to teach?" or "Who will be in the office?" or perhaps "Now I have to teach my students and you too?"

Using a School's Culture Helps Minimize Resistance to the Proposed Change Strategy

In Turnaround School, where the principal wanted everyone's help in establishing a professional learning community—of which she was the instructional leader—she needed to establish new, nonthreatening rituals that would be perceived as furthering everyone's values.

She arranged weekly celebrations where everyone would share a success he or she had that week with getting through to a student (as everyone valued student learning) and someone shared a particularly valued type of learning in which they had all engaged (since they valued their own learning). This new ritual was appreciated and demonstrated that even though there was change going on in the school, their values of learning were being furthered.

You want to assure people that their sense of the "world" will not change—in fact it will only improve. The key to this is to recognize what routines exist and how they are being affected and what values exist to further them and not inadvertently minimize them.

Analyze Your Own Tolerance for Participants' Resistance

A critical component of resistance analysis lies within you. In addition to trying to minimize resistance, you must anticipate the likely resistance and make a determination about whether you are willing to undertake the change strategy nevertheless. You have to do your homework. You have to take stock of how much resistance you are willing to encounter for the sake of getting the change initiative accomplished. You began to do this in your readiness assessment in Step 3, in the "willingness" assessment. How much resistance are you willing to take, if it comes to that, in order to accomplish the change initiative?

Common Mistakes to Avoid

Making mistakes might lead to more resistance instead of less. Be on the lookout for these mistakes so your efforts to minimize resistance won't be derailed.

Mistake #1: Not Accepting "Yes" for an Answer

A key concept that many leaders miss is that you sometimes have to accept "yes" for an answer *even if participants' reasons for saying "yes" isn't the reason you would prefer.* Often, the leader has one reason in mind behind the change goal, but individuals see different benefits and are willing to go along for those reasons.

This is fine. As long as people sincerely see positives in the proposed change and are willing to participate, it doesn't have to be for the same reason that the leader finds compelling.

Mistake #2: Making Too Many Changes at the Same Time

Human beings cannot handle multiple changes simultaneously. It is overwhelming. A simple illustration of this is to try to identity the nine possible different combinations of "A-B-C" without writing it down. Here's your nine seconds! If you were able to do it, congratulations. Some people can. Now try to identify the twenty-four possible combinations of "A-B-C-D," again without writing it down. Hardly anyone can do this. The point is that it is extremely difficult to hold three or four concepts in the brain simultaneously with all their possible permutations.

The same is true for change. We can handle one change and concentrate on it and two at the most. Once you ask people to engage in multiple changes, you will get resistance because it is simply too overwhelming.

Mistake #3: Not Planning Replacing What is Lost with Something Better

Resistance is likely to emerge in any change strategy because regardless of how positive the change, something is being lost. It may be that what is lost is "only" the comfort of old habits. There may even be recognition that those habits were counterproductive, nevertheless they are comfortable and will be missed until something better replaces

---

A State Minimizes Resistance to Establishing a New Set of Training Programs for Teacher Leaders

A state wanted to develop a set of programs for teachers who aspired to the new position "teacher leader." This action would involve the state education department, the university administrators and faculty, district administrators, and K–12 teachers. The state leader was aware that there might be resistance to this idea, but was willing to encounter it because it was important to develop a new career path for teachers who were not interested in becoming administrators.

In identifying the advantages and disadvantages, they found that university faculty members perceived more disadvantages while K–12 teachers perceived the greatest advantages. University faculty saw this as potentially "watering down" the current programs for aspiring administrators and lowering standards. They were also uncertain about what type of curriculum could be developed that was different from what already existed. How might this take away from what they were doing currently? Why change?

Most participating teachers, on the other hand, saw this as a chance to develop new skills and achieve promotions without having to become administrators. The group drew up a list of benefits to

(continued)

A State Minimizes Resistance to Establishing a New Set of Training Programs for Teacher Leaders (*continued***)**

the colleges and universities and nonprofit organizations, including a new ability to attract teachers who do not want to be administrators but are interested in furthering their careers through the teacher leadership pathway. The change would, in fact, permit them to raise the standards and content of their existing programs to focus on potential administrators, whereas this new program would accommodate teachers who wanted to advance, but did not want to be principals or assistant principals).

Once the first barrier was overcome, and university administrators and faculty came to believe that this program would be beneficial, another arose. Many faculty were resentful of the time that it would take to develop this new program. The change leaders remedied this resentment by seeking additional partners to shoulder some of the work.

The state joined a multistate consortium with others who were interested in developing a similar program. They divided up the work among six states and, together, have created a fourteen-course teacher leadership program, which has become a highly professional experience valued by those who were originally predisposed to resist it.

them. It is in that transition—when the "old" is out and the "new" is still untested—that loss will be felt by those affected.

The leader needs to recognize this loss and make sure that people have some time to mourn and so move on to concrete application of the new change as soon as possible. Loss can be mitigated by substituting something positive in its place. This is one of the values of the small early win tactic described in Step 5.

Mistake #4: Communicating Blame Whether Intentionally or Not

When communicating your change strategy, you want to take special care not to appear to be blaming anyone or anything. People will hear the request to change as blaming. Even if you are referring to decisions made before any of those present were there, they have been working in the current system and have some level of investment in it.

The two rules here are (1) never explicitly blame anyone—past or present—for why things require change, and (2) take care when you communicate the reason for the change strategy that your audience doesn't hear it as blaming. Test it out if you are not sure. When people feel blamed or undervalued, their resistance is palpable and hard to overcome. Once resistance festers, it can become part of people's history and even part of the organizational culture.

TOOL: RESISTANCE REDUCER

Your effort to minimize resistance is a three-pronged approach: (1) try to prevent resistance as much as possible; (2) minimize the inevitable resistance that occurs; and (3) decide how much resistance you are willing to tolerate in order to achieve your aims. The Resistance Reducer tool leads you through an analysis of all three aspects to help you make a plan to manage resistance effectively.

RESISTANCE REDUCER

Change Strategy Under Consideration: _____

_____

_____

Note that many of the forms in this book can be downloaded for free from the Jossey-Bass Web site. Go to: www.josseybass.com/go/spiro.

Effective Resistance Management = Preventing + Reducing + Tolerating

Be candid when completing this tool and try to think of concrete examples when answering the questions. Be careful when noting your ratings; the scale descriptions are not the same for all questions.

■　■　■

	RATING/SCORE

A. Preventing Resistance: To what degree can you prevent resistance before you start?

Answer the questions below by highlighting your score on the 5-point scale on the right.

1. Participants' readiness has been analyzed and activities are matched with that. Provision has been made to reanalyze to make midcourse corrections.	To a great extent　　Somewhat　　Not at all 　　5　　　　4　　　　3　　　　2　　　　1
2. It is recognized that people have different attitudes about change and ways of dealing with it. An effort is made to find out how the individual participants feel about change and develop strategies to make each feel comfortable. Surveys, interviews, and focus groups are used to gather information.	To a great extent　　Somewhat　　Not at all 　　5　　　　4　　　　3　　　　2　　　　1
3. There are many other changes going on at the same time as this one.	Not at all　　Somewhat　　To a large extent 　　5　　　　4　　　　3　　　　2　　　　1
4. Advantages and disadvantages of the change strategy from *participants'* points of view are identified up front. Strategies are developed to increase participants' perceived benefits and to decrease the negatives. The leader accepts that participants may buy into the change for reasons other than those that motivate the leader.	To a great extent　　Somewhat　　Not at all 　　5　　　　4　　　　3　　　　2　　　　1

Copyright © 2011 by John Wiley & Sons, Inc.

Copyright © 2011 by John Wiley & Sons, Inc.

	RATING/SCORE		

5. When communicating about the change strategy, the leader considers what people will hear as opposed to what he or she *thinks* is being said.	To a great extent	Somewhat	Not at all
	5 4	3	2 1

6. Participants feel blamed for the need to have change. If they had done their work better, change would not be necessary.	Not at all	Somewhat	To a great extent
	5 4	3	2 1

7. The leader is an active listener. He or she can turn off his or her own opinions and really hear others. The leader paraphrases the speaker often to confirm understanding.	To a great extent	Somewhat	Not at all
	5 4	3	2 1

Resistance Prevention Subtotal: Add your points scored for questions A1–A7. The total point score for "resistance prevention" is _____ out of 35 possible points. *The resistance prevention level is (highlight one): HIGH, MEDIUM, LOW*	High resistance prevention = 32–35 points	Medium resistance prevention = 21–31 points	Low resistance prevention = 20 points and below

B. Minimizing Resistance: To what degree can you reduce resistance as you go along?

Answer the questions below by highlighting your score on the 5-point scale on the right.

1. There is awareness that resistance comes with the territory in leading change, because participants are likely to experience loss and anxiety. Attempts are made to spot resistance at its earliest stages.	To a great extent	Somewhat	Not at all
	5 4	3	2 1

2. If some participants agree with the change in public—but talk against it in private—an effort is made to understand and address their points of view.	To a great extent	Somewhat	Not at all
	5 4	3	2 1

3. Resisters are engaged in collaborative planning for the change strategy, often teaming them with others who are genuine supporters of the change strategy.	To a great extent	Somewhat	Not at all
	5 4	3	2 1

	RATING/SCORE				
4. If the organization values competition, such tactics are used to motivate, but if there is no such value, competition is not encouraged.	To a great extent		Somewhat		Not at all
	5	4	3	2	1
5. Successes are celebrated with ceremonies and new rituals.	To a great extent		Somewhat		Not at all
	5	4	3	2	1
6. Learning is deliberately incorporated in most activities (even if it is informal or networking).	To a great extent		Somewhat		Not at all
	5	4	3	2	1
7. Participants believe that they are being treated fairly. For example: "negative balance of consequences"—whereby people who do the best job are "rewarded" by getting more to do without additional compensation—is avoided.	To a great extent		Somewhat		Not at all
	5	4	3	2	1

Resistance Reducing Subtotal: Add your points scored for questions B1–B7. The total point score for "reducing resistance" is _____ out of 35 possible points. *The reducing resistance score is: (highlight one): HIGH, MEDIUM, LOW*	High Resistance Reduction = 32–35 points	Medium Resistance Reduction = 21–31 points	Low Resistance Reduction = 20 points and below

C. Tolerating Resistance

For the leader: To what degree can you tolerate resistance when it cannot be prevented or minimized?

Answer the questions below by highlighting your score on the 5-point scale on the right.

1. I am totally committed to the change strategy and believe strongly that it will be beneficial. Therefore, I am willing to encounter whatever resistance I cannot prevent or mimimize.	To a great extent		Somewhat		Not at all
	5	4	3	2	1
2. I analyze the political power of those who are resisting to determine if they represent larger constituencies as opposed to individual issues. If resisters are individuals, I am prepared to tolerate their opposition.	To a great extent		Somewhat		Not at all
	5	4	3	2	1

Copyright © 2011 by John Wiley & Sons, Inc.

Copyright © 2011 by John Wiley & Sons, Inc.

	RATING/SCORE				
3. I avoid conflict at any cost. I like the work environment to be friendly. If there is too much resistance, I will back off.	Not at all 5	4	Somewhat 3	2	To a great extent 1
4. Resources and rewards are awarded on a competitive basis to those who support and further the change strategy if that helps move forward.	To a great extent 5	4	Somewhat 3	2	Not at all 1
5. If people are afraid they will lose their jobs and/or be underqualified for the new change strategy, I am prepared to support their development, but also prepared to encounter resistance from those who will be affected.	To a great extent 5	4	Somewhat 3	2	Not at all 1
6. If organizational values will remain the same or be furthered by the change, I emphasize that. If there is a deliberate attempt to change the values, I am prepared to encounter resistance.	To a great extent 5	4	Somewhat 3	2	Not at all 1
Resistance Tolerating Subtotal: Add your points scored for questions C1–C6. The total point score for "resistance tolerating" is _____ out of 30 possible points. *The resistance tolerance level is (highlight one): HIGH, MEDIUM, LOW*	High Resistance Tolerance = 28–30 points		Medium Resistance Tolerance = 18–27 points		Low Resistance Tolerance = 17 points and below

■ ■ ■

Tips for interpreting your results:

- If you are in the medium category, you might go further to see if you are "high" medium or "low" medium. If you are in the "low-medium" range, you might consider yourself "low" as you plan your resistance strategies.

- If you score "3" or below on any statement, you might consider developing a resistance strategy. You should prioritize having strategies for any 2s or 3s.

- On resistance tolerance, the following definitions might be useful: high means that the leader is willing to do whatever it takes to achieve the change strategy; medium means that the leader prefers little resistance, but is willing to encounter some in order to achieve the strategy; and low means that the leader wants a conflict-free environment and will not pursue a change strategy that encounters any serious resistance.

- A "low" rating for resistance tolerance for a given change strategy might cause you to reconsider pursuing that work.

Total Resistance Recap
(Transcribe from Your Totals from Sections A, B, and C)

A. Sub-score for resistance prevention:	_____ out of 35	Level: _____
B. Sub-score for resistance reducing:	_____ out of 35	Level: _____
C. Sub-score for resistance tolerance:	_____ out of 30	Level: _____
TOTAL RESISTANCE REDUCER SCORE:	_____ out of 100	Level: _____

High = 92–100; Medium = 60–91; Low = 57 and below

■   ■   ●

Implications for Going Forward

A. Resistance prevention strategies I might consider:

1. _____

_____

_____

_____

2. _____

_____

_____

_____

3. _____

_____

_____

_____

Copyright © 2011 by John Wiley & Sons, Inc.

B. Resistance reducing strategies I might consider:

1. _____
   _____
   _____
   _____

2. _____
   _____
   _____
   _____

3. _____
   _____
   _____
   _____

C. Resistance tolerance strategies I might consider:

1. _____
   _____
   _____
   _____

2. _____
   _____
   _____
   _____

3. _____
   _____
   _____
   _____

Copyright © 2011 by John Wiley & Sons, Inc.

> ## Determining Strategies to Prevent and Minimize Resistance
>
> *When using the Resistance Reducer tool, you can either project how others will respond, or you can ask participants to answer the questions themselves in sections A and B. The tool can be a nonthreatening way of getting direct feedback from those affected. Experience suggests that participants are almost always pleased to be asked sincerely for their feedback; however, the leader will get the most candid and useful information when responses are anonymous.*
>
> *Based on the data, you will be aware of participants' attitudes toward the change and what they perceive as advantages and disadvantages and can plan to build upon the former and minimize the latter. You will also be armed with an understanding of how the change message is likely to be heard and plan communications accordingly. You might want to repeat the administration of the Resistance Reducer tool at other points along the way in the implementation of the change strategies to make sure things haven't changed— or you adjust your resistance strategies if they have.*
>
> *In regard to your own resistance tolerance, you need to reflect carefully on your results. If you have a low resistance tolerance, you'll need to work on developing more. An effective change leader does seek to prevent and minimize resistance, but needs also to expect resistance and be prepared to deal with it in order to get the strategy accomplished. The most important change strategies often encounter the most resistance and the leader should be prepared for that.*

Note: You will find a completed sample Resistance Reducer in the Appendix.

TALES

Let's see how our four organizations planned for the resistance they expected to encounter and how that worked out.

IHHS Plans for Resistance from Staff Members at the Ministry of Education

The Ministry of Education of Pacifica was the main client and partner of IHHS in the reform of teacher training throughout the country. Nevertheless, the *individuals* within the ministry demonstrated serious resistance to actually seeing the work succeed. Would they be out of a job if the system changed? Even if they still were in their positions, would their power and influence be diminished? Would the change strategy result in a number of competing organizations, such as nongovernmental organizations, trying to do the training that the ministry currently performed?

There was much for ministry staff to worry about on a personal level even though the ministry supported the change strategy. The IHHS team leader was prepared to encounter such resistance because failure was not an option; nevertheless it was crucial to maintain the support of the ministry or the project could not be accomplished. It was important that ministry staff members understood the project and perceived more advantages than disadvantages.

A meeting was held where the objectives of the strategy were explained (after first analyzing what people were likely to hear as opposed to what the leader was saying). Then participants, who were low readiness, were each asked to list the advantages and disadvantages they perceived from the teacher training work. IHHS staff compiled the responses and now understood that staff members were most resentful that their subordinates in other parts of the country might wind up knowing more than they did about the new teacher training methods as the project moved forward.

Therefore, IHHS made a commitment to always brief ministry staff before doing anything. This mitigated anxiety and resistance to some degree until the project could demonstrate some results and momentum.

TUI Plans for Resistance from Staff Members of Potential Client Organizations

There were several cities that are interested in developing organizations based on the TUI model and existing nonprofit organizations that are interested in using TUI's assistance to improve their current programs. These cities and organizations came up as supporters in the stakeholder assessment.

However, the *staff members* at many of these institutions were concerned. Why did they need new programs? What's wrong with the way they are currently doing things? Why did anyone think that TUI's programs and services are better than theirs? Would they have the skills to conduct programs in the TUI way?

TUI addressed this potential resistance by emphasizing to potential client organizations the importance of adapting the programs and services to their local contexts. Only the local organization could do that, and the resulting program would look quite different from that used by TUI. Only the local organization could define the problem they were trying to solve. TUI never "told" people what their problems were.

The expertise of the local organization was indispensable to the quality and success of the product and service. This was true and, once demonstrated, convinced local organizations that the product or service was of value and that the local experts were the only ones who could make it happen. Resistance was minimal thereafter.

Changeville Assesses Resistance for the New Core Curriculum

The district leaders knew that academic achievement problems were serious and teachers were essential to addressing them. However, they also knew that they had to present the problem not only by articulating what they were hoping to change, but also by not creating a crisis of confidence in the schools about how they are currently delivering instruction.

They convened teachers and parents to try to understand the nature of the problem. They listed out what people might hear when the current messages were articulated. They took key words and phrases often used to frame the message about why schools need to change and then tried to anticipate resistance based on what people might hear. Here are some examples:

WHEN WE SAY:	THEY MAY HEAR OR THINK:
Twenty-first-century learning	Aren't we already in the twenty-first century?
Higher-order thinking skills	Educational gobbledygook
Technology	Computers
Regionalization or collaboration	School consolidation
Core curriculum	Content only (not rigor, relevance, pedagogy)

• • •

These exercises helped leaders identify areas of resistance and how they might minimize them at the onset by crafting their words carefully. Then they identified actual changes that were implicit in the core curriculum and identified the pluses and minuses of each of the major changes by framing them as gains and losses for those affected.

Turnaround School Plans for Resistance to the New Professional Learning Community

In developing a professional learning community (PLC) at Turnaround School, the principal wanted to establish collegial professional conversations that went beyond sharing ideas. She wanted all members of the school community to put ideas into action to improve school life for students and adults alike. However, in the past when she had brought up the idea, the staff as a whole seemed to be of the mind-set that "we already do that so why do we have to formalize it?" She decided that she had to alter her message to the reality of what people were experiencing, so she could propose how such a professional learning community could help everyone. So, the principal visited teachers and aides in their classrooms, safety officers at their posts, lunchroom workers in the cafeteria, and parents at the parent association meeting. She had individual discussions with various people about her idea. The notion of the professional learning community was modified according to what she heard.

The principal felt that she understood where people were coming from better and that school personnel respected her more. Because she had been "in the trenches" she understood how people were perceiving the world and was better able to propose activities that they felt were of value (and accept their suggestions for activities). She says that the quality of her conversations with school community members have changed and that they are more open to the PLC concept because they know that she is speaking from experience. She may even be saying exactly the same thing she said previously, but they hear her differently.

The principal remarked, "I had to put myself in the shoes of the different members of our community: parents, school aides, teachers, students, school nurse, dietician, custodian, educational assistants, assistant principals, and school safety officers. We worked on an appropriate message to deliver to all members of the community that would reduce resistance and bring about support. We were able to develop responses to questions and concerns we thought the different members would have regarding this new initiative."

WHAT ELSE IS NEEDED?

Once you have determined your approach to minimizing and tolerating resistance, there is another tactic at your disposal that will help you address any further resistance by inspiring confidence in the feasibility and benefits of the change strategy. This is the small, early win described in the next chapter.

Securing a Small, Early Win—

Turning the Tide Toward the Results You Want

It was so important that people started to see that we were on the road to something—and that isn't going away next year. Now everything we do is incrementally leading us to the larger goal. Keep showing them how what we're doing leads to the larger goal rather than being disjointed little pulses. This is important because there are no silver bullets; things always take longer, but now we all are traveling the same road.

—Principal of an early childhood center

TACTICS

As we know, change is a highly personal experience. Everyone participating in the effort has different reactions to change, different concerns, and different motivations for being involved. The results of change are long-term, but the change *process* is incremental and continuous. To bring people along with you, you need to give them evidence at each stage that the change will succeed and that is likely to yield positive results. That is especially true at the beginning, when skepticism about the benefits and possible costs is often highest.

In a sense, it is like the "loss leader" concept from the retail industry. In that case, retail shops offer serious bargains on some merchandise so people will come to take advantage of the low prices. Although the store may take a loss on those goods, once people come into the shop and see the quality of the merchandise, they may shop more…well beyond their initial reason for coming in. It is a way to demonstrate to people to see how valuable the products and services are—so that they come back for more.

An effective change leader deliberately plans for small, early wins that demonstrate concretely that achieving the change goal is feasible and will result in benefits for those involved. These should be planned actions within the overall change strategy—in the "action" column of the Strategy/Action Aligner. You should plan for achieving and documenting important results that are evident within the first month or two. Of course, all involved must agree that achieving this "win" would result in something positive—that is, meeting a common definition of "success"—and further the overall change strategy.

By doing so, you will inspire confidence that the rest of the initiative can be accomplished. However, it is critically important that once the early win is selected and announced, the promised results are achieved by the deadline stated. To do anything less would risk deflating confidence in the feasibility of the initiative.

Essential Elements

Within the first month or two of the implementation of the change strategy, you must produce a small result that meets a common definition of success. It must also be something tangible and observable, achievable, perceived by most people as having more benefits than costs, nonthreatening to those who oppose the strategy, and symbolic of a desired shared value.

Examples of Early Wins

Here are examples of some frequently used early wins.

Memorandum of Understanding

In the case of developing partnerships between organizations, an early win could be a "memorandum of understanding" between them. This legally recognized and symbolic document spells out the agreement between them and clarifies who will do what and the benefits that will accrue to each organization. In this way even those who might feel they are losing something by entering into the partnership also see what they are gaining. It should be possible to negotiate this in a month or two (particularly after using the collaborative planning process described in Step 6).

Pilot of the Larger Change Strategy

Sometimes the larger strategy will call for a service to be provided in several sites. An early win in this case might be an early tryout of an initial version of what is envisioned for the larger set of programs. The program then becomes "real," and has the added advantage of being subjected to review, revision, and improvement before going to scale. This is also a way to increase demand for the service.

(continued)

Tangible and Observable

The early win must be obvious to see; a real result that can be put on paper or made "real" in ways that everyone can observe. Using data is important here. You need to define specifically what the result will be (a product or a measurable change from X to Y). This will be the proof you present at the deadline to demonstrate that the win was accomplished.

Achievable

Above all, you must be able to do what you say you will do. You must be absolutely certain you can accomplish the "win" you put out there. If you fail to do this, you will do great damage to your cause. You will be proving the opposite of your intention—that this change is not feasible. So there is quite a lot riding on accomplishing the win by the deadline you announce.

Perceived by Most People as Having More Benefits Than Costs

Based on analyses you have done in the previous chapters, you should know what most people perceive as advantages from this change strategy. Your early win should further these gains so that people can see that the change strategy will actually result in benefits for them. In general, although not in all cases, some type of education or training program is usually perceived as a benefit as long as it matches the readiness of participants (that is, gives them skills/knowledge that they perceive they need and is not being imposed on those who believe they already have the skills or don't need them).

Nonthreatening to Those Who Oppose the Strategy

Because those who support the strategy are already on board, the audience for the early win is really those who might oppose the change or stand to lose something important to them as a result of the change. You will know who these groups are from the stakeholder analysis and the resistance analysis.

This will enable you to develop and implement an early win that, at best, will bring these folks on board and, at least, will have them understand that they should not be threatened by the change strategy. Another good way to do this is to try to develop an early win in an area that you have identified as exciting relatively fewer passions or greater urgency. These are the areas of least threat to anyone.

> **Examples of Early Wins**
> (*continued*)
>
> **A New Web Site**
> Organizations often design new Web sites to describe the organization's products and services. This can often be done within a month and is a concrete, observable deliverable that is perceived as important. It is the first line of communication with outside stakeholders.
>
> **Leadership Teams**
> Creating leadership teams can be done relatively quickly. Such teams empower participants with leadership roles and can not only result in improved decision making, but also serve as a step toward building trust and changing organizational culture.

Symbolic of a Shared Value

The early win is only of use if—after all these other considerations—it is perceived as important within the context of the organizational culture. It must be a symbol that says that important organizational values are being furthered by this win—and therefore by the larger change strategy.

Common Mistakes to Avoid

When it comes to early wins, mistakes are particularly difficult to recoup because achievement of these actions is meant to demonstrate the feasibility of the change strategy. It is, therefore, important to anticipate potential mistakes and avoid making them.

Mistake #1: Not Planning an Early Win

Leaders are often in a hurry to implement large-scale change—and in the process bite off more than is feasible. You need to build credibility first—then you will be able to succeed at larger ventures. Without a planned early win, you leave the perceived credibility of the change effort to chance.

Mistake #2: Not Using Data

You must use data to make sure you have the plan right (to test your assumptions about perceived needs and areas of fewer passions, for example). And set measurable objectives so you can point to the data at the deadline as proof of accomplishment.

Mistake #3: Keep Using Only "Early Wins" and Not Moving on to Larger Strategies after the Initial Success

A necessary point to bear in mind is that as important as it is to have an early win, this technique only works once—maybe twice! After you have established the momentum that an early win gives you, you need to capitalize on it and use your newfound credibility to develop the next, larger change strategy. Though successful, don't simply keep planning small, early wins—reach for the larger win.

Mistake #4: Insufficient Publicity

Another common mistake is not to publicize sufficiently. When you have your success, make sure everyone knows—or it will be of only limited use for your change strategy.

TOOL: EARLY WIN WONDER

The Early Win Wonder tool asks you and your team to brainstorm actions that have the specific characteristics of the tactic and discuss the degree to which each possible first action for your change strategy embodies as many of those characteristics as possible. You will notice that these characteristics are drawn from all the preceding chapters and tactics so the action chosen has the best chance for success as the turning point to having those affected genuinely buy into the change strategy.

EARLY WIN WONDER

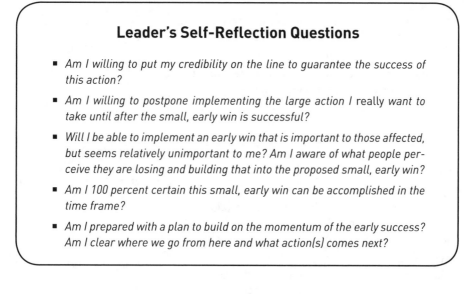

Leader's Self-Reflection Questions

- *Am I willing to put my credibility on the line to guarantee the success of this action?*

- *Am I willing to postpone implementing the large action I really want to take until after the small, early win is successful?*

- *Will I be able to implement an early win that is important to those affected, but seems relatively unimportant to me? Am I aware of what people perceive they are losing and building that into the proposed small, early win?*

- *Am I 100 percent certain this small, early win can be accomplished in the time frame?*

- *Am I prepared with a plan to build on the momentum of the early success? Am I clear where we go from here and what action(s) comes next?*

Overall Change Strategy:

_____

_____

_____

_____

Small, Early Win Action Under Consideration:

_____

_____

_____

_____

●   ●   ●

DOES THE PROPOSED ACTION MEET ALL ESSENTIAL CHARACTERISTICS OF AN EFFECTIVE EARLY WIN?	EVIDENCE (HOW?)
Importance Accomplishing this objective will meet the common understanding of what constitutes "success."	
Importance It is not merely "nice" to do, but necessary to move the work forward; the action is considered an urgent priority by most.	
Tangible and observable There is a transparent, observable outcome: either a specific work product or improvement measured by data.	
Achievable You are certain the change can be accomplished within the stated time frame.	
Perceived as having more benefits than costs to most people Individuals who will be implementing the action perceive benefits to achieving this "early win"— even if the benefits are not those that the leader articulates.	
Helps those affected deal with loss The action creates a positive substitute for what people perceive might be lost through the change strategy.	
Nonthreatening to opposing groups Groups that oppose the change would perceive benefits if this objective were accomplished.	
An area of relatively less interest The change is in an area that excites relatively and fewer passions by important stakeholder groups.	
Symbolic of shared values The program is an important symbol in the culture.	
Plans to publicize There are mechanisms to communicate the "win" broadly at the beginning and again at the deadline.	

> ## Determining Strategies to Secure Early Wins
>
> *Use a separate Early Win Wonder tool for each potential "early win" strategy under consideration. You can use it alone or with your planning group as a vehicle for brainstorming possible early wins and determining whether they meet all the criteria. The analysis may be done for what the group or individuals in the group might consider a win.*
>
> *The results can be used to rank the various strategies according to each strategy's likelihood of producing the desired early win. The tool can also help identify shortcomings in any strategy to increase its chances of succeeding. You might also use the data collected via this tool to brainstorm ways to take a potential loss and turn it into a win.*

TALES

Let's see how our four organizations framed small, early wins for their respective change strategies.

IHHS Selects a Corps of Sixty Highly Skilled National Trainers

The early win for the reform of the teacher training system in Pacifica was the recruitment and selection of a corps of sixty national trainers—senior, skilled educators who would serve as the lead educators to work with local groups of trainers in developing critical thinking instructional activities that could be shared with teachers. Although the eventual goal of the change strategy was to reform institutions throughout the country (universities and nonprofit organizations and perhaps the Ministry of Education), this overall change was quite threatening to those existing organizations.

Taking a small step such as selecting local educators who would serve as experts and trainers to the project furthered the larger goal, as training the sixty educators would bring capacity to the larger work when it began. No one could object to the training of such a corps of people. Symbolically this step was very important because it "proved" that senior, skilled, local educators were eager to be part of this new initiative.

The process of selection was highly competitive and prestigious. The criteria were published in local newspapers and education journals and in memoranda of the ministry. When the national trainer corps was identified—which happened on schedule—this was widely publicized in local newspapers and education journals as it was an honor for those individuals as well as for their region. Momentum was under way for the change strategy.

TUI Holds a Statewide Conference

In its effort to expand its services to new cities, TUI decided to hold a conference that would showcase their services and demonstrate how those services were of use to those in prospective new cities. Conference planning was done by first surveying the potential audience as to their needs; the content of the conference was based on TUI's products and services and how they responded to those needs.

The conference was widely publicized two months in advance and many people attended. The event demonstrated the value of TUI's products to a new market and was symbolic of the benefits that could be gained from their working with TUI.

Changeville Develops Core Curriculum in Third-Grade Mathematics

The districtwide group of teachers and administrators who had been meeting to develop the messages kept meeting to develop the first set of lessons—in mathematics. They announced that these first lessons would be available for tryout in third grade within a month and kept that commitment. The district newsletter on their Web site had announced that commitment and—one month later—announced the availability of the lessons for use in all schools. The district invited feedback on those lessons to be posted on the Web site, and the resulting discussion was rich. The lessons were revised in consideration of the feedback. The district community was eager to receive the next set of lessons and to participate in their development.

The superintendent put updates on schools' experiences with the new curriculum in his weekly newsletter to the district. A professional network was set up for teachers to share their experiences with the new curriculum and report back to the larger district community. The participating teachers created a survey that all teachers used after each unit of study to assess and report on student engagement with the lessons. The survey results were posted in Twitter fashion on the district's Web site and were made publicly available. These efforts at publicizing the success of this early win created much interest from the school community, including parents and students. As a result, new course development proceeded for all mathematics in all grade levels.

Turnaround School Holds the First Meeting of Its New Professional Learning Community

In its effort to develop a professional learning community, Turnaround School began videotaping (with the permission of the teacher) effective math lessons. The principal and the teacher discussed the lesson and then shared it with the community with the consent of the teacher. This was helpful to engage discussion and improve lessons and was also symbolic of the changed relationship between principal and teacher as the videos became the basis for shared learning rather than supervisory discussion. It was easy to do and did more to change relationships and promote learning than any large strategy could have done. And it paved the way to more shared learning schoolwide and an expansive professional learning community.

⬤ WHAT MORE IS NEEDED?

Now that you know the readiness of the participants, the positions of the stakeholders, and the resistance of the individuals involved—and there is a sense that the change strategy is feasible and beneficial—it is time to bring all the stakeholders together to develop the action plan.

Engaging the Key Players in Planning—

Achieving Collaboration Without Disintegration

Collaborative planning is the antidote to "groundhog day." Everyone was sick and tired of doing the same thing over and over again. For the first time everyone involved had clarity of purpose, results, and history of meeting's outcomes. Collaborative planning, in and of itself, is often an early win in a change process...a logical extension of the readiness assessment. This tool followed naturally because it established the agenda for the next meeting; set time lines to guide member actions; and most importantly, served as the historical account of the work. It became our action planner and data dashboard to determine where we were in the process.

—A district leader

TACTICS

Planning and implementing change are most effective when you involve people from diverse backgrounds and perspectives. Such broad participation empowers people by giving them a sense of control and ownership of the strategy and resulting changes. It also turns the change process into an enriching opportunity to examine multiple perspectives within the group, to gain an understanding and appreciation of differing viewpoints, to test long-held assumptions, to surface and purposefully channel conflict, and to build a network and team with other participants.

In short, collaborative planning is not only important for improving the strategies and developing buy-in for change. When done well, it has the added advantage of providing opportunities for learning and growth among participants. Recall from the tactics for reducing resistance that learning and growth are powerful motivators for most people and can help minimize resistance and accelerate your change strategy because doing so answers participants' question "What's in it for me?" Effective collaborative planning can help build a culture of learning in your organization in which risk taking, flexibility, and learning from mistakes are valued. Merely engaging in earnest collaborative planning is a symbol of the value of participants' expertise, openness to diverse perspectives, teamwork, cooperation, trust, and learning.

Essential Elements

A Climate of Respect Including Participants' Experiences—Both Good and Bad

Establishing a climate of respect is an essential foundation for this work. Even if a climate of respect and goodwill is not fully evident at the start, the process itself can help breed it, even among formerly hostile constituencies. Also, because participants come with prior experience, this must be taken into account in two ways. First, critical reflection of their experience should be incorporated into the resulting plan, thus adding value to the plan and meaning for participants. Second, you may first have to address participants' long-held skepticism of planning in order to gain their active, positive cooperation.

Diversity of Perspectives

The ideal collaborative process produces solutions that no one working independently could achieve. An effective planning group, then, is one in which people with diverse backgrounds and viewpoints are brought together, including people who may disagree with the prevailing wisdom but who will be called upon to support or implement the resulting program. An ideal size is from twelve to twenty participants so that there is enough diversity of perspective but also a small enough number to engage in an open exchange of ideas. If the group is larger than this, smaller groups can be broken out for discussion sessions.

Explicit and Enforced Ground Rules

Typical ground rules in an effective collaborative planning process may include that participants should (1) be specific; (2) state comments in a constructive manner rather than being critical, offering potential solutions when possible; (3) stay on topic; (4) keep discussions factual, not personal; (5) use data to support arguments; and (6) listen actively to each other. For low- and medium-readiness groups, the facilitator must enforce the ground rules. Even minor infractions, if ignored, can lead to disruptions of the group process.

In a high-readiness group, the participants themselves abide by the ground rules as a matter of cultural norm and enforce them as a matter of course. If the group wants confidentiality as a ground rule, you should add it; however, you cannot take responsibility for what happens outside the room to enforce that ground rule. So it should be clear that group members must self-enforce that rule.

Clarifying Actions Needed and Why, as well as
Individual Responsibilities and Deadlines

The result of this process is a detailed document which defines the mission, objectives, and strategies of the new policy or program. It delineates the activities which will be used, and assigns responsible staff with time frames for task completion. Importantly, it also provides documentation of the decisions made along the way—a historical record that may be important as others come into the process later. Such documentation can be a hedge against the disruptions often caused by turnover among planning group participants.

Ongoing Monitoring of the Plan

An implementation team can be created from among the original planners. They may be charged with overseeing the implementation and for making timely revisions as necessary. Just as with the other tools, it is essential that the Collaborative Planning Parameters be used in an ongoing way throughout the change process. In this way, midcourse corrections can be made as needed and continuous improvement achieved.

Your Role as Leader

The collaborative planning process is not easy or risk-free. The ego of the change leader or skepticism by participants can derail the process. Perhaps most consequentially, a leader may be tempted to water down or overgeneralize the decisions reached in order to achieve consensus or avoid conflict.

You will need to prevent the collaborative process from straying from the core goals of the change strategy. You want to make clear from the beginning which aspects are nonnegotiable. People appreciate not spinning wheels on something that cannot be changed. And you need to clarify that the decisions reached will be the best according to the data and not necessarily those of consensus. You also obligate yourself to explain the rationale behind the decisions that are reached to the entire group.

Common Mistakes to Avoid

Such collaborative planning is an excellent way to move the change process forward. Because it is so useful, one wonders why it is not used more often. Leaders are often leery of collaborative planning because it is easy to make mistakes that result in the group spinning out of control and reaching few agreements. However, once you are aware of the potential for the following factors to derail the process, you will be more prepared to lead collaborative planning effectively.

Mistake #1: Not Making Provision for Turnover in Participation

One aspect often omitted in the design process for collaborative planning is turnover in team members between meetings. This can lead to a lack of history and disruptive requests to reconsider previous team agreements and nonnegotiables.

You can plan for turnover by keeping an action planning sheet (with "reason for each decision" an important column), and list of attendees who agreed to the decisions.

You might also start the next meeting an hour later and invite the new participants to join you during the now vacated earlier hour for a status report briefing. This is respectful of them, of the time of the original members, so they don't have to hear a repeat of the last session, and brings them up to speed so that they can become productive meeting participants.

Mistake #2: Not Adjusting for Changes in Readiness

Although many groups begin as "low readiness," the success they will have together at the meeting should mean that their readiness improves during the course of the planning sessions. It is important to watch for this and test assumptions! Be prepared to substitute less-structured activities as the group becomes medium and high readiness. They will come to resent the structure as they know what they are doing.

Mistake #3: Not Really Being Open to New Ideas and Using "Collaborative Planning" as a Cover for a Predetermined Outcome

After a collaborative planning meeting, a principal said with "pride," "Well, the group came to exactly the outcome I planted. And they think it was *their* idea. So the meeting was a success." Assuredly, the group knows that the process was a sham designed to get them to say they bought into the leader's idea. It is better not to have any attempt at collaboration in that case and just say what it is rather than claim that your idea emerged from the group. No one is fooled and the "buy-in" is not real.

Mistake #4: Not Having Defined the Nonnegotiables

If you don't know ahead of time which aspects of the strategy cannot be changed, you will not achieve them and your group will spin its wheels debating points that later on turn out to be set in stone. This is a recipe for frustration and a real credibility drainer.

Mistake #5: Trying for Group Consensus If It's Not There

If you only accept ideas that have the agreement of the entire group, you will spend a lot of time trying to persuade outlier individuals. During the course of trying to get the widespread agreement, the likelihood is that the original concept will get watered down—becoming broader and broader—in trying to incorporate everything that is important to everyone. You are looking for the best idea and should not sacrifice those good ideas in order to incorporate everything needed for consensus. We saw in Step 4 that resistance is inevitable and, although you seek to prevent and minimize it, you must also have a tolerance for it when the hard call needs to be made. What is important is that you explain the rationale behind your decisions, particularly if there is no consensus.

Mistake #6: Not Having Ground Rules or Not Enforcing Them

If you don't have ground rules, no one will know what is expected of them—unless the ground rules are already part of the culture of a high-readiness group. Even worse is to have ground rules and not enforce them. The first time a ground rule is broken and unenforced, the group has the potential for anarchy—and the facilitator has lost the authority to bring it back.

Mistake #7: Not Getting Back on Track When Trust Is Broken

Trust is an important element in collaborative planning. If trust is broken, however, all is not lost. What is important is that the group gets back on track after the breach. Remember that this is political, not personal. You must always be aware of what you are trying to achieve and put aside any hurt feelings. Of course this is easier said than done!

You need to assess your power position vis-à-vis the trustbreaker and use it. But, once you are on an equal playing field, it is essential to resume collaboration rather than engaging in one-upmanship. The IHHS story at the conclusion of this chapter presents a good illustration of how this is done.

At the meeting itself, the leader can try to return to a trusting environment by focusing the discussion on something all group members agree on—perhaps the mission statement or the problem statement. There can then be a productive discussion of what each participant can do specifically to support that agreed-upon goal. Another way to regain trust and reclaim a productive atmosphere for the work is to use data. Asking participants to provide data to support their arguments brings the discussion to the facts as opposed to any lingering interpersonal issues.

TOOL: COLLABORATIVE PLANNING PARAMETERS

The Collaborative Planning Parameters tool asks you specific questions to consider when planning your first meeting and those to follow. It has been designed to use when you are at the initial stages of thinking through the planning process and the structure of the meeting(s) to achieve optimal results. The tool begins with questions that you should be prepared to ask yourself regarding your own motivations and preparedness to undertake this process. The tool ends with an "action planning sheet," which is the recommended alternative to keeping "minutes" and becomes the contract between you and the group regarding next steps and responsibilities, and also serves to ensure that everyone has interpreted the outcomes of the meetings similarly.

COLLABORATIVE PLANNING PARAMETERS

Copyright © by John Wiley and Sons, Inc.

Leader's Self-Reflection Questions

- *Do I have a problem to solve that participants will consider urgent and important?*
- *Can I demonstrate this with data?*
- *Am I genuinely open to new ideas?*
- *Have I identified the nonnegotiables and am I prepared to accept new ideas for everything else?*
- *Am I comfortable always enforcing every ground-rule infraction, regardless how "minor"? If I am not comfortable doing this, is there someone to whom I can delegate?*

Goal: To make the desired decisions while facilitating a learning experience for participants, without reducing the outcomes to only broad areas of consensus.

STRATEGIES	EVIDENCE
1. ARE THE RIGHT PARTICIPANTS AT THE TABLE? (SEE STAKEHOLDER STRATEGIZER)	
Those with the authority to make decisions?	
Those with important opposing voices?	
Those who represent important internal and external constituencies?	
Those who will ultimately do the work?	
2. READINESS ASSESSMENT AND STRUCTURE OF MEETING	
Is group readiness high, medium, or low? (See Readiness Rubric)	
If readiness is low or medium, is there high structure (for example: explicit ground rules, a written agenda, a mechanism for recording decisions, and use of writing to focus the discussion)?	
If readiness is high, does the group have sufficient autonomy?	
Are the group's shared values furthered by this meeting?	

STRATEGIES	EVIDENCE
If the readiness is mixed, are participants assigned to smaller working groups based on their readiness, with assignments containing structure in accordance with the smaller group's readiness?	
Are there plans to reassess the readiness at various points and adjust the meeting's activities accordingly if it has changed?	

3. PRE-WORK

Is there assigned pre-work that starts participants thinking, begins to develop a common language, and signals that this meeting will be substantive, serious, and a learning experience?	

4. CLARITY AND TRANSPARENCY OF MEETING OUTCOMES

Is there agreement that the topic of the meeting solves an important problem? Are data presented to support this?	
Is there a written statement of what outcomes are desired from the meeting?	
Are there benchmarks by which to measure success? (See Strategy/Action Aligner)	
Is there an up-front commitment to the end-time of the meeting?	
Is that commitment always met?	

5. ATMOSPHERE OF RESPECT

Are there light refreshments?	
Are all group members encouraged to contribute? How?	
Is participants' previous experience with such planning meetings acknowledged? And built upon if it has been positive; acknowledged and "unfrozen" if it has been negative?	

Copyright © by John Wiley & Sons, Inc.

STRATEGIES	EVIDENCE
Are participants heard? Are their opinions considered and incorporated into the discussion?	
Are decisions explained with the rationale behind them?	
6. GROUND RULES	
Are there clearly understood ground rules (written out for low-readiness groups; embedded in the culture for high-readiness groups)?	
Does everyone understand that the goal of the meeting is to get all the ideas on the table in a constructive way, but not to necessarily reach consensus? Understood that the results of the meeting will be transparent and the rationale for decisions explained?	
Is there a facilitator who will enforce the ground rules for low-readiness groups; and self-enforcement for high-readiness groups?	
7. MANDATE, CONSTRAINTS, NONNEGOTIABLES	
Are all nonnegotiables or mandates stated up front?	
Is there discussion of how to use those mandates to the advantage of the work? Is the message delivered considering what participants will *hear* as opposed to what the leader thinks is *said*? (See Resistance Reducer)	
8. EARLY WIN (SEE EARLY WIN WONDER)	
Is there an early win for the group within the first hour of the meeting (something tangible and positive that the group has accomplished together)?	
9. TEST ASSUMPTIONS OF WHAT HAS BEEN DECIDED	
Is there a clear, concise, and timely summary of what has been decided, who is assigned to do what and by when? (See Action Planning Sheet)	

Copyright © by John Wiley and Sons, Inc.

STRATEGIES	EVIDENCE
Do you test assumptions of agreement and not just assume that if there isn't active disagreement that everyone has accepted?	
Do participants have input in reviewing and revising those decisions? Does this happen within a day or two of the planning session?	

10. MECHANISMS FOR CONTINGENCY, MONITORING, AND REVISION

Are there check-in points throughout the meeting to ensure that participants believe the work to be on track?	
Are there specific ways in which modifications can be made as the work progresses after the meeting?	

11. INTEGRATION OF LEARNING

Are individual group members:	
Critically reflecting on their previous experiences and gaining insights?	
Learning new skills?	
Learning what the ramifications of these decisions are for practitioners who have to carry them out?	
Getting insight into other perspectives (such as program managers learning the perspective of the budget officer and vice versa)?	
Is the group as a whole:	
Solving a problem?	
Developing strategies that can be applied immediately?	
Learning how to be a team and the skills required?	
Forming supportive networks?	
Acquiring new resources (knowledge, people, and time)?	

Copyright © by John Wiley & Sons, Inc.

ACTION PLANNING SHEET

Instead of taking minutes, it is more effective to document the agreed-upon actions, their rationale, and who is responsible by what deadline. This stream-lined document (page 114) serves as the basis for ensuring that what needs to be done is clear and transparent. It also tests everyone's assumptions of what was really decided. It becomes a historical record and the basis for moving ahead with the actions needed.

Determining Strategies for Collaborative Planning

The Collaborative Planning Parameters are designed as a checklist for use by the leader or planning meeting facilitator to use in advance to plan the meetings and process by which the change strategies will be planned and implemented. The resulting data may be used by the leader or facilitator in conducting the meeting and making decisions during the meeting to ensure that the concepts presented in this tool are integrated.

It is suggested that you use an "action planning sheet" as shown to re-cord the specifics of what is to be done as a result of the discussions. This becomes a contract between the leader and the participants. It also tests the assumptions of what was decided. This is important because sometimes the leader or facilitator is so pleased to get a decision that you assume, often incorrectly, that everyone shares your understanding of what actually was decided. Shortly after the meeting, the draft action planning sheet should be circulated for comments and revisions by participants. The leader should then ensure that those responsible for various decisions implement them by the stated deadline.

Using the Collaborative Planning Parameters

A state wanted to explore developing a separate license and preparation program for "teacher leaders," because currently the only route to promo-tion and higher pay for teachers was to become administrators. The question was, "Could a new career path be opened to encourage great teachers to continue their practice at an even higher level?"

The planning process brought together all parties who would be involved with this reform. The group included representatives from the state educa-tion department, the state professional standards board, all universities in

(continued)

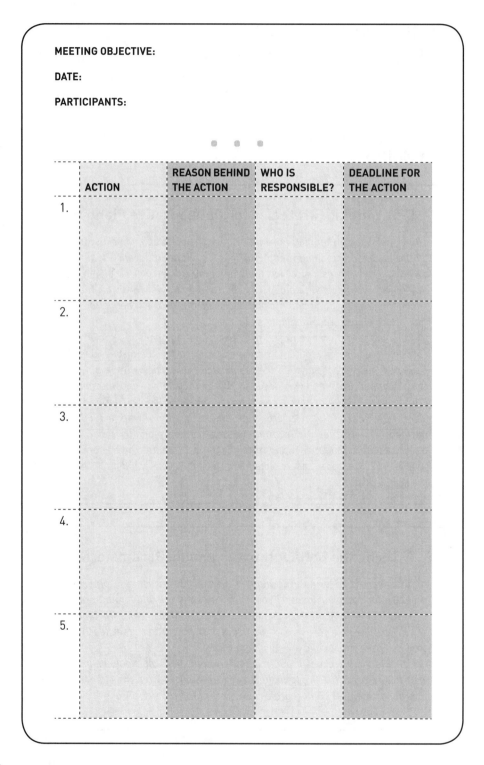

MEETING OBJECTIVE:

DATE:

PARTICIPANTS:

	ACTION	REASON BEHIND THE ACTION	WHO IS RESPONSIBLE?	DEADLINE FOR THE ACTION
1.				
2.				
3.				
4.				
5.				

the state with education leadership programs, key legislators, and representatives from several school districts and the supervisors' and teachers' associations. In all, there were twenty-five participants at the first meeting. The group, originally formed for the specific purpose, now meets three times per year. Following is a summary of the process they used, following the collaborative planning parameters.

Right Participants

The Stakeholder Strategizer tool was used to identify members strategically: school and district leaders, college and university leaders, the state Department of Education, the Education Associations (unions), and the statewide Professional Standards Board. The Education Professional Standards Board (the group with the power to make these decisions) gave the planning group the opportunity to develop the work collaboratively with them and have honored that commitment.

Readiness Assessment/Structure of Meeting

As one participant put it, "We learned the hard way that members' readiness is critical to the success of the work." Based on the Readiness Rubric, the readiness was assessed to be low to medium. Therefore, the leaders employed a highly structured approach.

High Structure and Clarity/Transparency

An agenda was sent to all participants in advance of the first meeting. Members commented that they like having this information in advance and feel they came to the meeting better prepared. The agenda was included with time designations for each item and an assigned timekeeper. There were ground rules, including a rule that although the group would try to reach consensus, they were looking for the best ideas even if everyone did not agree. If there was no consensus, the leader would make the decision, but the rationale for the accepted idea would be explained.

Pre-work

Pre-work was required: an assigned reading and a survey soliciting members' concerns, interests, or recommendations. At the meeting, all members were assigned to project work groups. Deliverable dates were established.

Use Writing for Focus and Structure

Writing served as a mechanism to facilitate participants' focus on specifics and gives them an opportunity to organize their thoughts before speaking. The planners used a "critical incident," where participants were asked to write responses to three or four assigned questions about a specific circumstance related to the given topic. This technique is particularly effective when the last

(continued)

question asks for a solution to the issue discussed. For example: "Think of a time in the past month when you experienced a particular problem related to our topic: (1) What was the problem? and (2) How was it ultimately resolved? How can it be prevented in the future?" Such an exercise can also be used to bring participants' previous experience into the discussion in a structured way.

Presentation of the Results of the Pre-Work Survey

The results of the pre-meeting survey were compiled and presented in the first part of the meeting. This served the need for data as well as for participants' focused thinking about the issues ahead of the meeting. It also signaled to participants that their input was going to be solicited and valued.

Atmosphere of Respect

Meetings were held at state parks across the state using a package plan that includes meeting refreshments, meals, lodging, and meeting rooms. At each meeting there was "share out time" and opportunities for all team members to provide input and explanation for their group work. At each meeting we celebrate work that has been successfully accomplished, a new evaluation system, for example.

In addition, new members who have little historical context for the work joined after the first meeting. We built in time to talk about the project in more detail so that new members could see how this work was critical to the overall goal.

Mandates, Constraints, and Nonnegotiables

The requirements for developing a teacher leader license were clearly stated upfront. Approval of the work plan developed at the first meeting—including the benchmarks and deadlines—was approved by the Professional Standards Board and became a nonnegotiable thereafter.

Assumptions of What Has Been Decided

An action planning sheet was drafted that documented what was decided at the meeting. It was sent to each member for review within two days of each meeting. It was revised to reflect group members' feedback and became the point of departure for the next meeting. Questions were clarified at that time and, before moving forward, the group voted on the actions via a show of hands.

Integration of Learning

During this planning process, members were exposed to materials that they were able to bring back to their jobs and use immediately. Everyone learned from real-life experiences—hearing from sitting principals, superintendents, and teachers. The leader commented that: "Using participants' personal examples, particularly the field people, helped everyone learn more about the realities of the work."

> *In fact, the group has become a professional learning community and a network that is connected by monthly face-to-face meetings, webinars, sitting together at other educational meetings, and through threaded e-mail discussions. There are informational presentations, mini-trainings, resource sharing, panel discussion, as well as meetings with resource people from different departments and agencies. All of this takes place on an ongoing basis.*

TALES

How have our four organizations used collaborative planning to plan and implement actions stemming from their change strategy?

IHHS Leads Collaborative Planning for an International Graduate Student Exchange Program

In pursuit of its change strategy to sponsor international graduate program exchanges, IHHS applied to be the administration organization under a Request for Proposals (RFP) issued by a government funder "to develop and implement an international graduate student exchange program for 150 students from designated Asian countries to come to study in the United States for total funding of $8 million." The RFP was given to only four organizations that were asked to work together to develop a program that could be implemented in a few short months. The only problem was that although they had to demonstrate how they would work together to get this done, each organization was to submit a separate, confidential proposal.

These four organizations were distinct institutions. Not only had they never worked together before as a team, there were times when they had competed against each other. Collectively they had experience and capacity (sometimes redundant) in the designated countries or in conducting international exchange programs. The funder had realized that no one organization had all the necessary capacity, and wanted them to work together.

The collaborative planning process, for this low-readiness group, was highly structured. It went well due to the high structure and the values shared across all organizations for improving the graduate education of students from the designated countries. The organizations also believed that this new program represented a new market for their services and that, should they do well in conducting this first set of activities, they might be retained in the future to do more work in this area for the funder.

Therefore, the collaborative planning went very well, with the groups analyzing the unique strengths of each organization and designing an action plan where each organization's strengths were emphasized. Where there were areas of redundant strengths, they negotiated which organization would carry out those activities. The four groups developed and agreed to a work plan. They also agreed that each organization would request $2 million, or 25 percent, of the available funding. Everyone left the planning meeting satisfied with the agreements that had been made.

But when the results of the competition were announced, there was a surprise. All organizations had submitted the agreed-on work plan; however, whereas IHHS and two other organizations had submitted a budget for $2 million, one had submitted a budget for the entire $8 million! To make matters worse, the funder gave that organization a disproportionate share of the funding. The organizations that had honored the agreement and requested $2 million received $1 million each while the organization that broke the agreement received $5 million.

So trust was broken, and—not only that, those who broke it were rewarded. Or so it seemed. Although one organization came away with the lion's share of the funding, they still needed IHHS and the other organizations in order to implement the plan. In effect, IHHS held power, if not funding. It was important that IHHS realized this. So, instead of lingering on the unequal funding dynamic, IHHS reminded the partners of the unequal power dynamic—that is, that the job could not be done without IHHS.

In the collaborative planning and implementation that took place subsequently, IHHS and the other agreement-honoring organizations were able to have the largest voices in how the work would go forward because the other organization was reluctant to cause further conflict. So the collaboration continued, but with a different dynamic—"trust but verify."

TUI's Collaborative Planning Process with Potential Users of Their Product

Once TUI had a group of interested clients, they had done some one-on-one product development with each. It was now important for the eight newly participating organizations to share experiences and approaches with each other, begin to form the virtual learning community, and to agree on any common language and program components. Therefore, the program planners and decision makers from the eight organizations were brought to a collaborative planning session with TUI.

The organizations' pre-work (and an early win) was a brief write-up of the status of the common project as implemented in their specific cities. This was posted on TUI's Web site as a first product of the virtual learning community. The meeting's participants were the "right" folks as they had both program expertise and decision making authority. The group was low readiness; these enthusiastic and skilled folks had never met together and had not previously collaborated with a national project.

The meeting was very productive for the first sessions as—through highly structured exercises—the group agreed on mission, shared experiences, and brainstormed solutions for one another's problems. The main problem arose in the later sessions when TUI proposed that the group should agree on some common project components and common language about their project, regardless of locale.

Three organizations balked at this—saying that their local situations were unique and they could not agree to common language or components. The program's developer also disagreed—for the opposite reason. She felt that the project should be replicated as is with no local adaptations.

The good news was that by this point in the meeting, the group was high readiness with participants willing to listen to the reasons given by their colleagues. After an hour of discussion, everyone saw the value of developing common "talking points"—as a core discussion guide. Anyone could add to these to reflect local realities. This was a breakthrough that enabled TUI to propose setting up a virtual learning community so that they could continue to share their experiences and brainstorm solutions between in-person meetings.

By this time, the group was willing to give it a try, and was eager to see the proposed draft "talking points" posted, which was a major decision made at the meeting. Enough was accomplished at this meeting to convince the organizations of the value of this mutual effort and they agreed to keep the learning community going.

Changeville's Collaborative Planning Process to Decrease the Student Dropout Rate

In pursuit of its change strategy of developing and implementing a core curriculum, a main action was defined as developing programs to keep students in school so they could have the advantages of the new core curriculum. The number of students dropping out of school was a serious problem for the district as demonstrated by the annual data produced. State funding was available to develop a new approach to this problem; all important stakeholders were brought together in a collaborative planning process over the three-year period. There were twenty-eight members of this group, which remained constant over the three years. The process changed during those three years as group members who were low readiness at the start became high readiness and the ground rules became part of the group culture.

The groups important to this process were: the superintendent and key Changeville district leaders (the chief budget officer, the head of the district's attendance, health and special education offices), two representative high school principals, two middle school principals, representatives from three community-based organizations providing after-school programs in high-needs neighborhoods, and representatives from the teacher and administrator unions and from the State Education Department. Once the data were distributed as pre-work, all concerned agreed that there was an important problem. However, it was a long-term problem and the group members were not optimistic that a single program could make a difference.

The First-Year Process

The activities were highly structured for this low-readiness group. This was the first time these stakeholders were in the same room and there was much to do before they could work together effectively. The pre-work had set the stage by documenting the extent of the problem with data. The group exchanged greetings over coffee for the first half hour and then set to business. The first order of business was the facilitator's sharing the meeting outcome (by the end of the second day, there would be draft guidelines for the new program) and the ground rules.

Participants then shared their critical analyses of experiences they had had recently with students who had either dropped out or who were prevented from doing so. They experienced an early win by agreeing on their shared value regarding children and education and they collaboratively agreed on a mission statement for dropout prevention work. All of this was done by highly structured exercises that were written by each member and then briefly presented.

The nonnegotiables were put on the table current district regulations were to remain active, there was a particular funding amount that could not be exceeded, and so on. Four smaller working groups were charged with developing no more than three strategies that would be within those parameters and bring them back to the larger group for discussion.

The turning point of the meeting occurred when three of the four working groups brought the recommendation that each school should have a "coordinator," whose job it would be to bring all the needed services together in the school in the service of those students who were at risk of dropping out. The budget officer, a member of the fourth group, objected strenuously, saying that the budget office never permitted funds to be used for "coordinators," as they were a waste of money.

A lively discussion ensued during which each group member passionately defended the need for such a coordinator in this case, given how numerous were the number of services and agencies that needed to be brought together in a holistic set of services for given students. At the end of the discussion, the budget director said that his eyes had been opened about the need for this position and he would agree to put it in the guidelines as allowable for funding. The rest of the group was stunned! From that point on, the credibility of the process was clear for everyone. The budget director had learned a great deal and a decision had resulted that made a real difference for those who had to implement.

The Results from the First Year

The planning process resulted in a set of guidelines that gave schools discretion to choose among menu options to create the program that best met the needs of the school and its students. One of the most important outcomes of the meeting, in addition to the development of the guidelines for the new program, was that in interviews conducted with the participants five years after the last meeting, every single participant claimed, "It was really my idea that was the main reason for the success of the program." This type of buy-in has been essential for the success of the program, and demonstrates how the leader has to leave his or her ego at the door as everyone emphasizes his or her contribution to the ultimate result.

The Third-Year Process

The group stayed together for three years, meeting annually for review and planning and twice within each year to consider midcourse corrections. After the first meeting, this group of diverse stakeholders came together over their shared values and goodwill—and the success of early wins. After the first year, they had become a high-readiness group. The meetings were "structured" whereby the desired objectives were agreed on and the group devised the methods by which they wanted to approach the task.

They were able to request the resources that they needed (mostly experts of different types) for the work from the district and then presented the results of what they had done to the superintendent and district staff on the last day for review and any required revision. The program is now over twenty years old, clearly sustained within Changeville.

Collaborative Planning at Turnaround School

The principal of Turnaround School conducted the first meeting of the professional learning community by identifying a key problem (the need to improve mathematics instruction) and used the collaborative planning process to come up with new ideas.

She says that the simplicity of the steps takes the emotionalism out of decisions that are made, easily makes it imperative that many people be involved in the planning and decision making, and it makes certain that they have a "next steps" plan using the Action Planning Sheet whenever they leave a planning session.

They have used this multiple times as they have worked through the restructuring of the school for the next school year.

■ WHAT ELSE IS NEEDED?

Now that you have your plan, and the genuine buy-in required to make it happen, you need to make sure that your change strategy will last and is not just a one-time event. The next chapter provides tactics and tools to help make this happen.

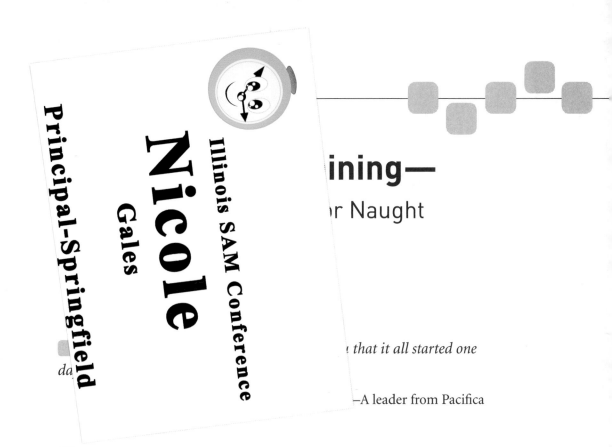

ining—

r Naught

that it all started one
da

—A leader from Pacifica

Planning for sustainability at the beginning of the strategic plan-
ning process was the most important thing we could have done. We
wouldn't have thought to do that without the tools.

—A state leader

TACTICS

From the beginning of an initiative and throughout its life, scale and sustainability are key aspects to consider. Even if you succeed at your change strategy, it means little if the resulting program or practice does not spread or live on after the initial success.

Scale involves not only "breadth"—that is, widespread adaptation of a program or practice—but also "depth," that is, evidence of penetration and high quality in all programs that result from the change. Too often "scale" is associated only with "spread" and the resulting programs may be numerous but watered-down versions of the original. For successful scale to occur there needs to be, first of all, a clear understanding of the core elements of the original model. As the program or practice spreads, you must strike the right balance between preserving the essential properties of the original and allowing for and encouraging local adaptations.

Scale is hard to achieve even for highly defined and effective programs. What is brought to scale must be a proven model and its effectiveness should be demonstrated with data.

The program or practice needs to have a niche beyond anything currently available or it won't have a market. When possible, the new program or practice should make use of and be combined with existing infrastructure and programs. You have to determine just how much scale is required to have the impact you are seeking and, of course, to assess the readiness for participation of the various stakeholders. An important aspect of creating scale is to provide training and assistance for new sites or users and supporting them all by uniting them in an ongoing network or community of practice where they can share experiences and learn from each other.

Sustainability involves the long-term staying power of the resulting program or practice. This involves enduring laws, skilled staff, communications, ongoing evaluation and continuous improvement in infrastructure, partnerships, and organizational capacity. It involves funding that is reallocated from other programs of less importance. All this is necessary but insufficient. To ensure that a program or practice is truly "in the water supply," people's attitudes and behaviors need to change, culture needs to change, and key stakeholder groups must embrace the program as their own. Often, sustainability may *begin* with laws and policies and funding. But to last, a change must become embedded in the culture, and in the attitudes, values, and behaviors of those most affected by it.

The Real Goal—Change in Behavior and Culture

Although we most often think of scale and sustainability as referring to a program or practice, it should be noted that the most enduring impact is change in people's behavior or organization culture. This was the reason you identified and pursued your change strategy at the beginning. You were trying to solve a problem and thought this change strategy would do that. The problem isn't solved by a *program*; it is solved by changing *behavior and culture.* That is, both individual behavior and the behavior of the entire group. Sometimes creating or changing laws or position descriptions can be an early win—and a good place to start because they get people used to the new norms of behavior. But more is needed so that people continue the behavior and the values become embedded in the culture.

An example of this is the no-smoking regulations that have led to the recognition of the importance of a non-smoking environment. It is unthinkable to smoke in the workplace now, for example, whereas not so long ago that was common practice. It is not universal, of course, but the values and practice of smoking have gone beyond regulation to common practice.

What you are looking for is a measurable increase in impact based on the spread of a program or practice. An example can be seen from an elementary school principal who participated in a program where he had an operations manager to handle noninstructional functions, freeing him to spend more of his time on improving instruction.

A Program Embedded in the Culture

In one mid-sized urban school district, one of the only programs unscathed by recent major budget cuts was the academy for training school leaders. When asked why this program survived the ax, a senior official noted that principals, assistant principals, and teacher leaders in the district now expect such training throughout the year to help them do their jobs and to prepare them for future advancement. A district leader commented: "They [the school leaders] don't even think about it. They don't even know who is responsible for making it happen. They only know that they participate in training and it helps them get through the year. They expect it. We couldn't possibly take it away without major complaints." That is a culture change in the district. It promotes the sustainability of the program and also of the behaviors that result from participating in the program.

His percentage of time spent on instruction improved from 25 to 90 percent in three years. So the "program" sustained and had a measurable impact.

Even better, however, is that this principal later assumed the same position at a different school—one that did not have this program. And the time he spent on instruction was still way above the norm at 65 percent. He commented that as a result of previously having the operations manager, he was now aware of what he was *supposed* to be doing to improve instruction and was finding the time to do it. In other words, his concept of the job had changed and his behavior had changed, and these changes outlived his participation in the program. Other principals who have been participating in the program are also changing their behavior—and principals who are not in the program are hearing about the success of those who are and may choose to participate in the future.

Essential Elements

Achieving scale and sustainability is difficult and involves planning from the very beginning of the initiative. However, keeping your eye on these fundamental aspects can help the effort last well into the future.

The Program Serves a Need and Has a Market

In order to be scaled and sustained, the program must address problems that are perceived as needs. Decision makers, planners, participants, and funders must believe that the program to be scaled and sustained serves an important purpose and has the potential for broad impact. Only then will they be willing to contribute time, skill, and resources to the effort in an ongoing way. An effective change leader tests the assumption of need by conducting market research to find out if the assumed need is there in reality—and to identify any roadblocks that may be apparent.

Core, Nonnegotiable Elements Are Identified

The foundation of both scale and sustainability is to distinguish the core, nonnegotiable elements of the program from those that are less critical to replicate precisely. Often the developers feel that the program should always be implemented exactly as it was originally. In order for scale and sustainability to take root, there are only a few elements that are essential to enact exactly as the originators did things. Everything is not of equal weight. It is very important to identify those elements that need to be replicated faithfully from everything else, which needs a local touch.

In this regard, it is also necessary to distinguish the program elements that are required from those that are nice to have, but not imperative. This is regardless of whether they are replicated from the original program or developed locally. Evaluation can play an important role in distinguishing the core elements. Because you want to sustain programs that have been successful or have that potential, evaluation can tell you which elements were most important for the successful outcomes to date.

The True Cost of the Program Is Determined

Make sure you figure out the true costs of running the program and also be aware of the revenue it is generating or the amount of funding you have from government sources, contracts, grants, or philanthropic contributions. Sustainability is not achieved by getting more funding. You need to make sure you have enough funding to run the program. If you are running a financial deficit between your operating expenses and your revenues, getting more funding may only make that gap larger.

Hard Choices About Resources Are Necessary

There is seldom "new" money, even for worthwhile programs. The largest potential source of funding comes from reallocating what you already have. Programs that are sustained by shifting funds from other programs of lesser priority have a greater likelihood of enduring since they become part of the system and their priority has been demonstrated. It takes courage to make such decisions, and that is what is called for in this situation: the leader must be willing to reallocate resources in order to scale and sustain the change strategy.

> **Resource Reallocation Is Possible with Political Will**
>
> One state demonstrated its commitment to training for school principals by setting up four local leadership academies in different parts of the state. They contained a common core of program elements but were largely based on the needs of the local school districts. Once these academies were in operation, the leaders of these districts and the program participants were enthused about the programs.
>
> As a result, the state reallocated millions of dollars from other purposes to the creation and operation of leadership academies in all the high-needs districts across the state. The reallocation of funds enabled them to achieve scale of this proven program quickly and sustainably.

A variation on this theme is to scale and sustain a program by incorporating it into an existing program—to the enhancement of both. An example of this is the nonprofit organization that employed a cadre of coaches who provided one-on-one support for city leaders. When they wanted to scale and sustain a newer program that counseled leaders in time management, they trained the existing cadre of coaches in this skill rather than hire additional "time coach" specialists.

Scale and Sustainability Are Planned from the Beginning

Although you can see whether your efforts at scale and sustainability have been effective near the end of your change strategy, the leader needs to plan for it from the beginning. The actions needed for long-standing and long-lasting change need to be planned and implemented with that end in mind. You must dig the deep roots for change at the beginning for them to take hold.

The Plan Is Monitored and Revised Along the Way

You need to plan for sustainability at the beginning of your change strategy, but be open to new pathways to sustainability as you implement. The partners and institutions you create along the way—which didn't exist when you planned your sustainability efforts—might turn out to be important for the endurance of the change strategy in the end. In addition, other variables are likely to change. The downturn in the economy in 2009 presented financial obstacles that were not around in 2000, for example. Leadership changes happen that affect your work—both positively and negatively. Agendas of partner organizations may change. Organizational priorities may change. Such factors have to be constantly addressed in the revision of your initial scale and sustainability plans.

The Next Generation of Change Leaders Is Trained

If you are going to have truly long-lasting change, there is a good chance that those involved with the original planning and implementation will no longer be around in future years as the change is sustained. Even though no one likes to think about this (and we all like to think we are indispensable), if the change is to endure, the next generation of change leaders must be trained.

A Principal Training Program That Has Stood the Test of Time

Ten years ago, a school district understood that nearly two-thirds of its principals would be retiring within three years. The need was urgent to train successors who would be able to maintain and even improve the high level of performance of those schools. Therefore, the district set out to develop training programs for those who aspired to be principals—and succeeded! The talent was developed and succession was pretty seamless—and the quality of education continues to be high.

The now ten-year-old training program is still going strong, despite losing its initial source of funding after five years. In fact, it has been scaled to another eleven districts in the state through partnership with a local university. The original architect of the program is the only person remaining from the original design team; however, he is in a supervisory position now. He credits the endurance of the program with how it has been embedded in the district's policies and culture, and the large number of current principals who have been trained by the program and therefore share its techniques and values.

But mostly, he says, the key element for its enduring success has been that the original planners "trained the next generation of change leaders" intentionally from

(continued)

Staff Turnover and Transitions Are Well Managed

Change of personnel in key positions is a frequent impediment to scale and sustainability. Incoming staff often either do not understand the program fully or deliberately diminish it because it isn't "theirs." Although the potential for disruption is present, there are ways to minimize the impact of transitions. Of course, the more advanced knowledge of turnover in personnel the better. There can be a transition plan and a period of overlap between the tenure of the incumbent and the successor; this is the ideal.

However, turnover often happens with little notice and there is no planned transition. There is still much a leader can do to facilitate a smooth or seamless flow to the work. Several tactics described earlier in this book can be used to good effect; engagement of a wise variety of stakeholders ensures a constituency for the program that makes it hard to dismantle. Sometimes the new personnel have already been working on the change strategy from another position in an involved group.

Early wins and benchmark data provide evidence of success or potential. And, as mentioned in the collaborative planning tactic, it helps to document decisions together with their rationale so that anyone coming in later can understand what was done previously.

Coping with transitions is challenging, but as with all the leading change tactics, disruption can be minimized through awareness of the issues and attention to the step-by-step processes.

Common Mistakes to Avoid

Barriers to successful scale and sustainability may result in programs and practices that do not last. Paying attention to what can go wrong may help you steer clear of these derailers.

Mistake #1: Not Identifying the "Core" Elements Up Front

This is the key aspect of scaling and sustaining, but possibly the most overlooked. It requires the leader to analyze the program or practice for those indispensable aspects that make it work and must be implemented with fidelity. There are two common mistakes in this regard, in addition to just not doing this at all: (1) not being able to identify those aspects that are the drivers of the successful program and why, and (2) identifying so many "core" aspects that there is no discretion left for local adaptation. Everything is not so important as everything else. Making these distinctions is critical.

Mistake #2: Being Either Too Prescriptive or Too Locally Adaptive

Finding the right balance between fidelity to the original program or practice and adapting it for local context is the heart of the issue for effectively achieving scale. It is natural for the originator of the program or practice to want to see it implemented as designed; it is also natural for those on the receiving end to want to revise it to meet their own unique needs. It is important to have negotiations between prescription and adaptation up front. Of course, this is only possible if the limited number of core elements have already been identified and put on the table.

> **A Principal Training Program That Has Stood the Test of Time** (*continued*)
>
> the beginning. This includes the principals and other school leaders who have been trained, the faculty from the partner universities, and the next generation of district leaders. It is these leaders who have ensured that the funding is there and that the programs have become part of the district's infrastructure and its ongoing requirements for up-and-coming and current leaders.
>
> The district leader who successfully scaled and sustained programs over the past nine years commented, "I am the only person remaining from the original planning and design team. I was a junior staffer nine years ago and I am a senior official today. But I am surprised as I look around and see that I am the only one left!" Developing additional change agents has been the key to the scale and sustainability of this leader training program.

Mistake #3: Not Scaling to a Sufficient Number of Sites for the Impact You Seek

There is not a single answer to the question, "How many sites do you need for scale?" You must think this through for each change strategy. How much spread will give you what you need for impact so that your program is not thought of as merely good in a limited number of places, or suitable only for sites with certain characteristics?

Mistake #4: Equating "Sustainability" with "Funding"

Most often people think that if they have (or do not have) the funding, that is the beginning and end of sustainability. Although funding is certainly an important component, it is only part of the story. Sustainability is achieved through culture change, human capital improvements, and organization structures.

Mistake #5: Thinking That "Self-Perpetuating" Is the Same as "Sustaining"

Remember that the goal is to sustain only those programs or practices that are of high quality, value, and impact. Unfortunately, often "sustainability" becomes an end unto itself. That is to say, the aim is to keep things going as is because that's what people know, or people's jobs are at stake, and so forth. Not everything deserves to be sustained. Only programs or practices that have proven value should be seen in this light. Self-perpetuation is not a worthy goal—it only reinforces business as usual.

Service-providing organizations like IHHS and TUI often seek to build sustained capacity within their client organizations rather than self-perpetuate their own involvement after a given period of time. They often have a rule of thumb that during the first year of a three-year project, they contribute 80 percent of the human capital while the client contributes 20 percent. The second year the levels of effort are equal at 50 percent each.

By the third year of the project, the expectation is that the initial percentages are reversed, with the client contributing 80 percent and the service provider putting in only 20 percent. After the third year, the client organization should be able to fully implement the work without assistance. In this way, there is planned sustainability for the client and a lack of self-perpetuation by the service provider.

Mistake #6: Planning Well, but Not Implementing Well

There is a huge gap between planning and implementation when it comes to achieving scale and sustainability. Even when there is a well-done plan, "the devil is in the details" when it comes to actually making it happen. You must consider not only how to plan for scale and sustainability, but for the difficult job of implementing those plans and revising them for midcourse corrections. It is important to distinguish between what is "on the books," versus what is really "on the ground." Therefore, the Scale and Sustainability Score Sheet tool presented here examines planning and implementation separately for each category so you can see the full picture of your scale and sustainability efforts to date, identify gaps, and determine how to go forward.

TOOL: SCALE AND SUSTAINABILITY SCORE SHEET

Scale and sustainability planning should happen at the beginning of the work or as soon as possible once the program or practice has been identified. The Scale and Sustainability Score Sheet tool may be used by the leader, with a team, to determine what is needed to ensure the eventual scale and sustainability of the change strategy. It is important to engage a team because seldom does any one person have all the perspectives needed to perform this assessment holistically. The ratings and evidence provided by completing the tool should give the leader a good idea of the specifics needed in planning and implementation that are likeliest to result in scale and sustainability.

The tool is designed to be used for programs or practices that have evidence of high quality or demonstrated potential. There are six steps: (1) assess the leader's readiness to plan for scale and sustainability, (2) define the program or practice that you want to scale and sustain, (3) identify its "core" elements, (4) analyze what you currently have for effective scale, (5) analyze what you have currently for effective sustainability, and (6) develop actions to address the gaps you have identified.

SCALE AND SUSTAINABILITY SCORE SHEET

Be candid when answering these questions and try to think of evidence to support your ratings.

Note that many of the forms in this book can be downloaded for free from the Jossey-Bass Web site. Go to: www.josseybass.com/go/spiro.

Step 1: Assess the Leader's Readiness to Plan and Implement Scale and Sustainability

- Am I willing to identify the several program elements as core or non-negotiable?

- Am I willing to let go of the notion that every part of the program is essential, and encourage adaptation of the noncore elements based on local needs?

- Can I make the hard choices to reallocate current resources to the scale and sustainability of the current program (if it is a higher priority)?

- Am I prepared to be opportunistic? Am I willing to revise and adapt the plan when circumstances change?

Step 2: Describe the Program or Practice Resulting from Your Change Strategy That You Are Considering Scaling and Sustaining

What is it? Why is it important? How do you know it is of high quality and valued? What results are anticipated? How might behavior change in the long run?

_____

_____

_____

_____

_____

_____

_____

_____

Copyright © 2011 by John Wiley & Sons, Inc.

Step 3: List the Core or Nonnegotiable Elements of the Program or Practice

1. _____

_____

_____

_____

2. _____

_____

_____

_____

3. _____

_____

_____

_____

4. _____

_____

_____

_____

5. _____

_____

_____

_____

Copyright © 2011 by John Wiley & Sons, Inc.

Step 4: Scale

To what extent have the following elements been incorporated into your program or practice?

FOR PLANNING (P)	FOR IMPLEMENTATION (I)
5 = A comprehensive plan in place that all stakeholders "own"	5 = All aspects have been fully implemented
4 = A comprehensive plan in place that most stakeholders support	4 = Most aspects have been fully implemented
3 = A plan in place with some support	3 = Some aspects have been implemented
2 = A partial plan with modest support	2 = Few aspects have been implemented
1 = No plan	1 = No aspects have been implemented

	SCALE CATEGORY	RATINGS			
		(P)	(I)	TOTAL P + I	WHAT MORE IS NEEDED FOR SCALE?
I.	A model with demonstrated effectiveness or promise				
II.	A program or practice not only in more places, but with high quality and depth of implementation in all those places				
III.	An underlying set of principles with action steps leading to the model's desired outcomes				
IV.	A justified hypothesis and/or research that supports the rationale behind the model				

Copyright © 2011 by John Wiley & Sons, Inc.

Copyright © 2011 by John Wiley & Sons, Inc.

	SCALE CATEGORY	RATINGS			
		(P)	(I)	TOTAL P + I	WHAT MORE IS NEEDED FOR SCALE?
V.	Replication of identified core elements of the original model with contextual modifications; ownership by local adapters				
VI.	High demand; fills an acknowledged need; market has been demonstrated				
VII.	A large number of supporters beyond those first to embrace the strategy				
VIII.	Structures or mechanisms through which the model can be spread				
IX.	Personnel who are skilled in the model and can train others				
X.	A detailed implementation plan with monitoring and continuous improvement built in				
SCALE Total (P & I) out of 100 →					
	Total	(P)	(I)	(P+I)	

Step 5: Sustainability

To what extent have the following elements been incorporated into your program or practice?

FOR PLANNING (P)	FOR IMPLEMENTATION (I)
5 = A comprehensive plan in place that all stakeholders "own"	5 = All aspects have been fully implemented
4 = A comprehensive plan in place that most stakeholders support	4 = Most aspects have been fully implemented
3 = A plan in place with some support	3 = Some aspects have been implemented
2 = A partial plan with modest support	2 = Few aspects have been implemented
1 = No plan	1 = No aspects have been implemented

SUSTAINABILITY ELEMENT	(P)	(I)	TOTAL P + I	WHAT MORE IS NEEDED FOR SUSTAINABILITY?
I. LAWS, REGULATIONS, POLICIES				
a. Supportive laws or regulations in place				
b. Institutionalized outcomes of the change (i.e., procedures, position descriptions, curriculum requirements)				
I. AVERAGE SCORES FOR CATEGORY				
II. KEY INDIVIDUALS				
a. Key stakeholders engaged				
b. Little active opposition				
II. AVERAGE SCORES FOR CATEGORY				
III. EXTERNAL PARTNERSHIPS				
a. Key organizations engaged				
b. Key organizations perceive the program or practice as furthering their own goals				
c. Union contracts support the program or practice				

Copyright © 2011 by John Wiley & Sons, Inc.

Copyright © 2011 by John Wiley & Sons, Inc.

SUSTAINABILITY ELEMENT	(P)	(I)	TOTAL P + I	WHAT MORE IS NEEDED FOR SUSTAINABILITY?
III. AVERAGE SCORES FOR CATEGORY				
IV. INTERNAL ORGANIZATIONAL CAPACITY				
a. Organizational goals furthered by the change				
b. Well-defined procedures and systems for implementation				
IV. AVERAGE SCORES FOR CATEGORY				
V. HUMAN CAPITAL				
a. A clear and legitimate procedure of succession for those leading the effort				
b. Mechanisms are in place to ensure that transitions to new staff are as seamless as possible				
c. Staff with the skills and knowledge to implement the new program or practice				
d. An institutionalized system for training personnel in the skills needed by the program or practice, including training the next generation of change leaders for this initiative				
V. AVERAGE SCORES FOR CATEGORY				
VI. FUNDING				
a. Ongoing funding from diversified sources (no reliance on a single source of funding)				
b. Distinction between what is essential from what is *desirable*; and full, ongoing funding for all essentials is in place				
c. Reallocation of resources to the new program or practice including cutting funding to programs that are not working well				

SUSTAINABILITY ELEMENT	(P)	(I)	TOTAL P + I	WHAT MORE IS NEEDED FOR SUSTAINABILITY?
d. The "real" costs of the program are identified. It is known what the program actually costs when the core elements are fully implemented				
e. The new program is incorporated into existing programs and thereby leverages the funding from the existing programs so no new funding is required				
VI. AVERAGE SCORES FOR CATEGORY				
VII. CULTURE				
a. Program or practice furthers existing values and norms				
b. Favorable attitudes toward the new program or practice				
VII. AVERAGE SCORES FOR CATEGORY				
VIII. CONTINUOUS IMPROVEMENT				
a. Continuous gathering of data to support the achievement of the change goal				
b. Provisions for monitoring, learning lessons, and consequently making midcourse corrections				
VIII. AVERAGE SCORES FOR CATEGORY				
IX. COMMUNICATIONS				
a. Ongoing communications mechanisms including use of media and public relations				
b. Transparency of progress to all constituencies				

Copyright © 2011 by John Wiley & Sons, Inc.

SUSTAINABILITY ELEMENT	(P)	(I)	TOTAL P + I	WHAT MORE IS NEEDED FOR SUSTAINABILITY?
IX. AVERAGE SCORES FOR CATEGORY				
X. EVALUATION (SUMMATIVE)				
a. Assessment of the program's or practice's accomplishments versus planned outcomes after a specified time period; identified lessons learned				
X. AVERAGE SCORES FOR CATEGORY				
SUSTAINABILITY GRAND TOTAL → Total the Averages (Out of 100)				
Total	(P)	(I)	(P+I)	

Step 6: Determining Strategies for Scaling and Sustaining the Results of the Change Strategy

You will have a rating for each scale and sustainability element. This should enable you to ask the following questions:

1. *What more do I need to plan to get scale (in order of importance)?*

_____

_____

_____

_____

_____

2. *What more do I need to implement to get scale (in order of importance)?*

_____

_____

_____

_____

_____

Copyright © 2011 by John Wiley & Sons, Inc.

3. *What more do I need to plan for sustainability (in order of importance)?*

_____

_____

_____

_____

4. *What more do I need to do for sustainability (in order of importance)?*

_____

_____

_____

_____

_____

Note: You will find a completed sample Scale and Sustainability Scoresheet in the Appendix.

TALES

How have our four organizations used collaborative planning to plan and implement actions stemming from their change strategy?

IHHS Achieves Scale and Sustainability with the Graduate Exchange Program

The international exchange program for graduate students from the Asian countries was a success in its first year. All students were selected and placed in U.S. university programs within the ambitious time frame. All four organizations worked together efficiently to bring this about; as a result, the program was funded again during the next fifteen years and still endures as of the writing of this book. Approximately two thousand students have participated, including people who have become senior government officials in their countries.

For IHHS, this program has increased its organizational capacity to administer international exchanges, and it has developed a division of exchanges for this program as well as the others it now runs. The program has been sustained and scaled to other exchanges for other parts of the world and in other content areas. In many ways, this sustainability is surprising. In the beginning, IHHS was part of this initiative to get a foot in the door to develop a market in Asia—a loss leader that would lead to additional work in the region. The pleasant surprise is that the program itself has legs. All these years later, IHHS has a sustained organizational division that does nothing but education exchange programs and is well known for its expertise in this area.

IHHS also achieved scale and sustainability with the Pacifica Teacher Training Reform. That story is told in the next chapter because it was achieved only through a midcourse correction of the approach.

TUI Expands Its Services to Other Cities, Which Have Adapted and Sustained Them

During the past five years, TUI has worked with thirty-five school districts that have replicated the core elements of TUI's program, but made significant local adaptations. There are common "talking points" and an ongoing community of practice that meets periodically and shares learning via a virtual community. The work has not been easy and has had many bumps in the road; primarily around the questions of the balance between the core elements and local adaptation. Nevertheless, TUI has achieved and sustained its change goal to become an organization providing programs and services well beyond the city of its location. It has diverse funding that includes government contracts, fee-for-service from other cities, and association fees. The organization has carefully calculated the cost of providing each of the core services so that there is no gap between operating expenses and revenues. The fee they charge for services fully covers their expenses.

There is a new infrastructure, agreed to by TUI and the districts, that clearly defines the role of each entity. TUI provides defined support to the districts and monitors across districts to ensure fidelity of the implementation of the core elements. Each district runs the program locally, developing local adaptations that best fit its needs.

Changeville Sustains Districtwide Dropout Prevention Program and a New Curriculum in Mathematics

Dropout Prevention Program

The planning process described in Step 6 took place from 1984 to 1987. The program has been sustained in Changeville in regulation and practice since 1984. The funding that was in jeopardy of not being reauthorized in 1984 has become a permanent allocation from the state. The program has been institutionalized, scaled to all middle and high schools in the district, and sustained—now as part of the district's culture. The participants in the collaborative planning process designed the program to have six core components that all schools had to have; however, they could choose from a menu of ways to deliver these components or could propose their own methods to address those mandated components.

This provided adherence to the main elements with enough flexibility in implementation to lead to scale and sustainability. The dropout rate in the district during this time has been reduced, and although this single program cannot claim total credit, it certainly has been part of the reason.

Mathematics Curriculum

Changeville schools now use new mathematics curriculum in all grade levels. There are volumes of lesson plans that teachers may use, or they may create their own using the learning objectives and curriculum provided by the district. Last year, students made strong test score gains in mathematics, providing encouragement that this strategy was working and would continue.

Turnaround School Has a Functioning Leadership Team and an Ongoing Professional Learning Community

The professional learning community has been operational in Turnaround School for the past year—not yet long enough to claim sustainability, but a good start. The school has organized the class schedule so that teachers have common preparation periods that enable them to meet to discuss the various matters on the agenda of the professional learning community. There is space on a private school Web site for teachers to post documents and record comments. Some teachers are even using such techniques with their students.

The learning community has produced a small volume of lessons in each subject area and teachers are using them, exchanging classroom visits to observe the lessons, commenting on them online, and suggesting revisions. The working groups take the suggested revisions into account when finalizing the lessons. Other common problems of practice have been identified and discussion groups have been held about ways to address them, including conducting action research to collaborate on addressing the problems.

The learning community has used school data to identify the lowest-performing students and brainstorm ways to assist those students as a community. They have used assessment of instructional practices assessment to determine school improvement priorities. The principal has hired a coach for the school who assists with the facilitation of the learning community and the identified professional development. The professional learning community is now part of the school's culture. All signs are that it will continue.

WHAT ELSE IS NEEDED?

Now that you have a scaled and sustained change strategy, did it indeed address the original problem sufficiently? Even if scale and sustainability have been achieved, monitoring and further revision are often required.

Monitoring and Continuously Improving—

Taking Advantage of the Changes You Will Encounter

You have to keep using the tools continuously. We use them over and over.

—A district leader

TACTICS

Because change is by nature continuous, and outcomes hard to predict, it is difficult, if not impossible, to get everything right in the initial plan. It is of utmost importance to keep an eye on the implementation of the strategy, analyze what is going on, and make revisions as you go along. As you strive to reach each "destination," you will probably find that you need to alter your path en route.

Essential Elements

You are ahead of the game if you understand that you are not done with your change process once you have your plan with assignments and deadlines. You will be further ahead if you build the following elements into that ongoing work.

Revisions Made Based on Reflection and Experience

It isn't enough to plan; you have to implement and revise as you go along. The best plan is only a guide. Because change means doing something different, no one can predict with certainty what will work well, what might work better, or what might not work at all. Leading change can only be done effectively when the leader uses a continuous process of planning, implementing, monitoring, and revising the actions.

A Specific Process for Monitoring Progress

The goal is to catch what isn't working early on and to make needed revisions before it becomes a major problem. Because the initial plan will have delineated benchmarks, these should be taken seriously and assessed through data as well as the perceptions of process. A process for making this happen should be developed and made operational. Such mechanisms might include regularly scheduled meetings or virtual space with blogs where perceptions and lessons can be shared in real time and an ongoing dialogue can take place.

Drilling Down from Generalities to Specifics

The more specific the leader can be during planning and implementation, the better. It is far easier to elicit agreement to general concepts than to specific actions—but note that things that sound good in generalities often fall apart in implementation. Often the leader is grateful to "escape" with any sort of agreement, and stops short of questioning whether there is general consensus or genuine, deep commitment. Of course, you need the latter. Real agreement and commitment will enhance implementation and drive the discussion toward specifics, even though the discussions will be more difficult. This approach will pay off later.

> ## "Details" Can Derail Even a High Readiness Group
>
> State officials were planning comprehensive education reform strategies. They engaged a wide variety of stakeholders and all agreed to the elements needed to bring about their set of initiatives. They conducted a readiness assessment and stakeholder analysis and used collaborative planning to develop a long-range plan. There were several early wins. Everything seemed to be on track until they got into the details of implementing the plan.
>
> Although everyone had initially agreed that "teacher leadership" should be an important part of the plan, it became apparent that there were differing points of view on the specifics. These disagreements endangered the implementation of this important part of the plan. Disagreement centered on the question of whether there should be a new certification for teacher leaders.
>
> *(continued)*

Constant Awareness of How Things Have Changed and Anticipation of Coming Changes

You need to think several steps ahead and not assume that the circumstance will remain as it is now. Just when you think you have your action steps defined, you may be blindsided by something major that has changed in the larger environment that will prompt you to redefine what you need to do.

Baseball managers provide a good example of being proactive about changing strategy based on changing circumstances. When pitching changes are made during the game, managers make other adjustments in their lineups based on the new situations. Of course, some do this better than others!

Some examples of changes that may affect you include new members on the board; new staff members; an economic downturn; a new, competing organization; or a new grant opportunity. As these events happen, the effective change leader recognizes that subsequent adjustments are likely to be needed. It is far better to be proactive in anticipating these changes than to have to scramble after the fact. Just ask any baseball manager who leaves a pitcher in the game too long.

An Ongoing, Holistic Picture of What Is Needed to Carry Out the Strategy

It is certainly hard work to put all the leading change steps into action. If you have used the tools to plan the tactics, you probably think you have most or all the contingencies well thought out; however, you have to keep reassessing all the tactics as you implement change. What is encouraging is that, after a while, the steps become natural to your thought process and you will do them automatically in your head. Until then, it is important to use all the tools frequently.

Common Mistakes to Avoid

As with the previous steps, there are potential pitfalls that are easier to avoid when forearmed.

Mistake #1: Viewing Modifications to the Original Strategy or Plan as "Mistakes"

Most of us like to think that once the planning is done, we can move on to the next phase of implementation. If we did our job well, the plan will be a good blueprint. Only if we didn't do our job well would we have to admit mistakes and "go back to the drawing board." That isn't the case with situations of change. Your plan should be a living document, a natural reflection of the change process. It is unfortunate to assume that something is awry when, during implementation, you find that you need to change the plan. In fact, revisions are to be expected. Do not hold onto your plan because otherwise people will think that you made a "mistake." You may well miss opportunities to improve your chances for success.

Mistake #2: Not Setting Benchmarks and Not Using Data

The benchmarks in your plan are your guideposts. They must be taken seriously and monitored in an ongoing basis. Benchmarks must be quantified so

> **"Details" Can Derail Even a High Readiness Group (*continued*)**
>
> Although group readiness was high in general, readiness for this discussion was low. Questions arose such as "If a person is already in a formal teacher leader role in a district, will this person have to go back and do coursework to earn a certificate?" Rather than proceed as planned, the group stopped the work and took the time to surface all the specific questions. They then added new members to the group— teacher leaders themselves— who were asked to provide detailed information and perspective to raise the readiness of the larger group to discuss this issue. The teacher leaders' information and perspective resulted in approval of the new teacher leader certification.

that you, the members of your team, and the larger community will all agree that success is well defined by these measures. Then it will become transparent to all what the status is as you implement the plan. You can use this as the basis to suggest midcourse corrections.

Mistake #3: Trying to Monitor by Yourself

Remember that leading change effectively requires multiple perspectives. No matter how good a leader you are, you cannot be in all places and experience all perspectives. You need a team of people who will continuously assess progress and share their perceptions and lessons learned.

The effective leader forms the group, provides training for them, and sets up ongoing mechanisms to facilitate reflection and sharing. This serves as input for the revision of the original plan.

TOOL: THE 3 R'S: REVIEW, REVISE, REPEAT

Leader's Self-Reflection Questions

1. *Do I deliberately and regularly review implementation for places where further changes are needed from what was planned?*

2. *Do I view "mistakes" as opportunities to learn and consequently develop new strategies and actions?*

3. *Am I willing to consider additional actions that may be more effective than the initial actions in implementing the original plan?*

4. *Do I rely too heavily on people who "think like me"?*

5. *Is there an opportunity to productively bring new voices into the work?*

■ ■ ■

TACTIC	MIDCOURSE QUESTIONS YOU SHOULD BE ABLE TO ANSWER BY USING THE TOOLS	POSSIBLE ACTIONS TO TAKE
1. Determine your change strategy and make your plan.	Is/was this the right change strategy to address the problem you were trying to solve?	If yes, keep going; if no, rethink and revise the change strategy.
2. Assess and improve the readiness of those affected.	What is the current readiness of the group or key individuals (as opposed to what it was at the beginning)? Has the readiness improved? Or has readiness declined once the specifics of the work were apparent?	Revise your collaborative planning design to reflect less structure if the readiness level has improved. If the readiness level has not improved, keep high-structure group strategies. Demonstrate how the program is furthering organization values.
3. Analyze the stakeholders.	Are the right groups actively engaged? Are any groups missing? Have the positions of key groups changed on this strategy since the beginning?	Add missing groups. Deepen the engagement of important groups not currently actively involved. Delineate clear roles for participating groups for next tasks.

Copyright © 2011 by John Wiley and Sons, Inc.

TACTIC	MIDCOURSE QUESTIONS YOU SHOULD BE ABLE TO ANSWER BY USING THE TOOLS	POSSIBLE ACTIONS TO TAKE
4. Minimize resistance (and maximize your tolerance for it).	What level of resistance has been encountered? Can it be minimized further? If resistance is present, are you still convinced that the strategy is worth continuing?	Continue to restate the messages to the audience's ears; if resistance is still present and the strategy is still important, engage supporters and continue the work. Emphasize the success of early wins.
5. Secure a small, early win.	Have we secured your early win? Is there momentum for the strategy now?	If the early win has been achieved, publicize and capitalize on momentum. If the early win has not been achieved or if it did not work, quickly plan a new "win" for the next month.
6. Engage all those affected in collaborative planning.	Are the right groups at the table, including the opposition? Is the structure of sessions commensurate with the readiness of the group? Is there agreement on the central aspects of the strategy?	Add missing groups; make better use of under-utilized groups. Add more structure or lessen the structure as appropriate. Get agreement on the main aspects of the strategy before moving forward. Develop implementation plan and monitoring mechanisms.
7. Plan for scale and sustainability and implement the plan.	Are the core elements right? What gaps remain regarding planning for scale and sustainability? What gaps remain regarding implementing scale and sustainability?	Add or take away strategies as appropriate. Develop actions to fill gaps. Continuously revise plan as appropriate during implementation.
8. Build in ongoing monitoring and course corrections.	Are the actions working as hoped to address the problem? What midcourse corrections are needed in change step tactic?	Modify the strategy (even if implementation is successful) if not solving the original problem. Develop midcourse corrections based on analyses from using the tools. Analyze lessons learned that may inform future change strategies.

Note that many of the forms in this book can be downloaded for free from the Jossey-Bass Web site. Go to: www.josseybass.com/go/spiro.

Copyright © 2011 by John Wiley and Sons, Inc.

TALES

In Step 7 we learned how each of our organizations had scaled and sustained its identified change strategy. This result did not happen without midcourse corrections. Following are examples of such revisions that were made during the implementation of each organization's change strategy.

IHHS Revised Its Sustainability Approach for the Pacifica Teacher Training Reform

From the beginning of the initiative, the plan had been to scale and sustain the teacher training reform through the Ministry of Education. The concept of a "public-private partnership" underlay the strategy. IHHS would provide content know-how and system-building expertise in concert with the Ministry of Education. The ministry would provide local expertise and—what was important for scale and sustainability—the authority to enact policies throughout the country to which all universities, districts, and schools had to adhere. The idea was for IHHS to help change the education system from within.

In the beginning, this underlying premise seemed to be working. The ministry identified excellent candidates to be "teacher trainers," worked with IHHS to develop workshops for them, and proposed legislation to make the job of "teacher trainer" an official position with a higher salary than teachers received.

As the work went forward, however, the legislation encountered resistance and the ministry backed away from this commitment. It became apparent that no policies would change in support of the work. Therefore, IHHS had to recognize that this partnership would not result in scale or sustainability. The organization did, however, perceive that there was another route, one that was unanticipated at the beginning.

The national trainers who had now been developed and certified as qualified by IHHS and the Ministry could become the purveyors of scale and sustainability. The sixty trainers, even though they were not in licensed positions, were trained to be agents of change. With some additional training and support, many of them went on to develop their own organizations, which provided the planned teacher training throughout the country. These organizations still exist today and are built into the fabric of districts' teacher training systems throughout the country.

Had IHHS not been willing to recognize that the original strategy was not likely to work, and had not developed an alternative approach, there would have been no scale and sustainability. And the midcourse correction was unknowable at the beginning of the work. The action of training national trainers developed only after the project had begun; IHHS could not have predicted how talented and entrepreneurial these trainers would become. But using this unintended positive consequence led to the sustainability of teacher training reform in Pacifica.

TUI Changed the Content of Its Early Win Strategy

TUI had planned to hold a conference as their early win. There were several cutting-edge leadership topics about which they thought their potential clients needed to know more. As discussions with clients progressed, however, it became apparent that the issues that TUI staff thought to be important were not on the radar screen of the potential audience. Rather than hold the conference as planned, and hope that the strength of the content would persuade the audience of the value of the content, TUI stepped back, postponed the conference, and formed a planning group of clients.

When the conference was held, a month later than originally scheduled, it was a success. The sessions were a mixture of topics perceived of interest and value by the clients and some content that TUI felt was important for them. The clients were satisfied, TUI established credibility, and no one cared that the conference took place a month later than planned.

Changeville High Schools Reworked Class Rosters in the Middle of the School Year

Changeville school district had developed courses and lesson plans to implement the new mathematics curriculum across the grades. They had piloted them successfully and thereby achieved an early win. Teachers shared their experiences through meetings and through virtual meeting space. Hopes for the new curriculum were high.

However, midyear analysis of the high school data revealed disappointing results. Teachers liked the new lessons, but student engagement measures and test scores were not improving. Reflecting on this situation, the district implementation committee realized that they had not given criteria to the schools regarding how to program students for these new courses.

There were prerequisites needed for certain courses that had not been factored into students' course assignments. When schools monitored results in December they realized that many students had been misprogrammed for certain courses. Taking midcourse action, the high schools made changes in course rosters over the winter break and reassigned students to different math courses for the spring semester. This provided a fairer test of the new curriculum and did not force the district to wait until next year—and was of real benefit to the students who were now in their correct course placement. It was a lot of work to reprogram the students, but the effort was worth it. Had the revision not been made, the initiative might have been scrapped for lack of results.

Turnaround School's Principal Changed His Main Action

Recall that the principal's dilemma at Turnaround School was how to involve the entire school community in developing new ways of engaging students in learning. One initial action the principal took was to teach a course to high school students. It was an elective for a small group of seniors. The principal thought that she would benefit from direct engagement with students, but, most important, she also believed that teachers would come by to observe her class and that such visits would generate discussion about effective teaching. Unfortunately this didn't happen. Teachers came by only infrequently and were uninterested in discussing this specialty class. They didn't feel it applied to them or their classes.

After one semester, the principal decided to regroup and engage the leadership team to determine what actions could be employed to better achieve the aim of involving the school community in discussions of teaching and learning. That was when the strategy of developing a professional learning community was born. Each member of the team became responsible for leading specified types of learning experiences. Teachers shared their best practices and struggles and became critical friends to each other. Only by letting go of the strategy she initially developed did the principal revise the strategy to achieve the goal.

WHAT ELSE IS NEEDED?

Now that we have completed the eight steps, what have we learned and what more is there to do? It is time to go back and complete the workplan begun in Step 1 and implement your plan—always with an eye toward continuous improvement.

Using the Tactics and Tools to Make a Real Difference

HOW TIMES HAVE CHANGED

In the 1970s and 1980s, when professors and organizational training instructors taught management courses, there were several "tips" often given to participants. Among them were:

> *It is helpful to know your management style and how it matches up against the "ideal."*

and

> *If you aren't sure what to do, rely on precedent. You can't go wrong by repeating what has worked in the past.*

Neither piece of advice would be given today. In fact, there are at least three ways in which things have changed significantly in the past few decades for those looking to make things happen.

In the first place, the emphasis is now on "leadership" as opposed to "management"—that is, the more visionary, inspirational, mobilizing, and influencing skills rather than the managerial scheduling, reporting, budgeting, and coordinating roles.

Second, we now realize that there is no such thing as a general "style" that works in all situations. Leading change requires adaptation to the situation at hand.

Finally, in today's world relying on precedent is problematic. Leaders need to anticipate and predict. Even what works today may not work tomorrow. In fact, all effective leadership today involves leading change.

OUR WORLD NEEDS EFFECTIVE LEADERS OF CHANGE

Our need for effective leaders is urgent. Opportunities for progress abound as never before—if we can harness the new technologies and global connectivity for worthwhile purposes. This book has attempted to empower those who want to make a positive difference in today's world. One does not have to be in a formal leadership position to drive positive change. The tactics and tools in this book can make the change processes more transparent, specific, and easy to navigate. And the stories about change leaders let us know that it is indeed possible to bring about the changes we seek if we are intentional and persistent.

We hope that after reading this book you will feel empowered and inspired to take the following measures.

Make the Hard Decisions Around the Identified Priorities

It is so important that you are able to identify your priorities and make your subsequent decisions accordingly. Some things are more important than others and deserve more attention and resources. You need to determine your nonnegotiables, core program elements, key stakeholders, and reallocate your time, human resources, and funding. These priorities must be transparent and must also allow for adaptation in all areas other than the nonnegotiables. They must be measurable, with defined benchmarks and processes to assess progress.

Anticipate the Opposition and Resistance You Will Inevitably Encounter

Be prepared for the opposition and resistance you will undoubtedly encounter and know that leading change often requires courage. Nevertheless, you can plan to minimize this through assessing readiness up front, including the opposition in planning, building in short-term wins and ongoing learning experiences, communicating effectively, and encouraging local adaptation.

Scale and Sustain What Works

Make sure you have actions that will spread, stick, and last. Plan up front to enable your program or practice to endure—understanding that funding is important, but not the only aspect you must secure. Also key are policy changes, human capital, communications and—most of all—embedding in the culture.

Continuously Monitor, Revise, and Make Mid-Course Corrections

Keep your eyes on the ongoing implementation and collect and analyze data as you go along. Don't do this alone, but with your team. You need multiple perspectives to learn lessons as you go along.

* * *

Leading change is certainly complex, difficult, and continuous. But this set of skills is among the most important any leader can develop. The stakes are high, the risks are great, but the chance to have an impact on improving people's lives is substantial. When done well, these tactics can help you help others in meaningful ways. Ready, set, go! And then reassess, revise, and go again!

SAMPLE COMPLETED TOOLS

A number of the rubrics and tools in this book are available for free download from the publisher's web site. To access these downloadable files, go to www.josseybass.com/go/leadingchange and type in m4i3sy8.

READINESS RUBRIC

Copyright © 2011 by John Wiley & Sons, Inc.

Change Strategy Under Consideration: *HHS Teacher Training System Reform*

_____

_____

Note that many of the forms in this book can be downloaded for free from the Jossey-Bass Web site. Go to: www.josseybass.com/go/spiro.

SECTION A: LEADER'S READINESS

Readiness = Experience + Skills + Willingness + Shared Values

Be candid when completing this tool and try to think of concrete examples when answering the questions. Be careful when noting your ratings; the scale descriptions are not the same for all questions.

	RATING/SCORE

A. Experience: To what degree do you have previous experience with change in general and with this type of change in particular?

Answer the questions below by highlighting your score on the 5-point scale on the right.

Question	Rating/Score
1. Have you successfully led change in any organization before, especially an organization similar to the current one?	**Many times** 5 (4) **Once or twice** 3 2 **Never** 1
2. Have you successfully led change in this organization before?	**Many times** 5 4 **Once or twice** (3) 2 **Never** 1
3. Have you led change in any organization *unsuccessfully*?	**Many times** 5 4 **Once or twice** (3) 2 **Never** 1
4. Do you have previous successful experience in the technical content area of the change strategy (i.e., management consulting, curriculum development, teaching science)?	**A great deal** (5) 4 **Some** 3 2 **None** 1
5. Have you been able to "unfreeze" participants' previously negative experiences with change and motivate them to take a leap of faith now?	**Always** 5 4 **Sometimes** (3) 2 **Never** 1
Experience Subtotal: Add your points scored for questions A1–A5. The total point score for "experience" is _19_ out of 25 possible points. *Therefore, my readiness level regarding experience is (highlight one): HIGH, (MEDIUM,) LOW*	High readiness = 22–25 points	Medium readiness = 15–21 points	Low readiness = 14 points and below

A. Required Skills: To what degree do you have the required skills and knowledge for this change strategy?

Answer the questions below by highlighting your score on the 5-point scale on the right.

	RATING/SCORE		
6. Do you have expertise in the content required by this change strategy? If not, do you have confidence in the expertise of others on your team?	**A great deal** (5) 4	**Mostly** 3 2	**Not as much as desirable** 1
7. Are you skillful at leading change?	**Very skillful** 5 (4)	**Somewhat skillful** 3 2	**Not at all** 1
8. Are you aware of what you do not know and are you candid about it?	**Always** (5) 4	**Somewhat** 3 2	**Seldom** 1
9. Are you willing to learn together with the participants when the skills and knowledge are just emerging?	**Always** (5) 4	**Somewhat** 3 2	**Seldom** 1
10. Are you an active listener (i.e., paraphrasing, waiting 9 seconds for response after asking a question)?	**Always** 5 (4)	**Somewhat** 3 2	**Seldom** 1
Required Skills Subtotal: Add your points scored for questions A6–A10. The total point score for "experience" is _23_ out of 25 possible points. *Therefore, my readiness level regarding skills is (highlight one):* HIGH, MEDIUM, LOW	High readiness = 22–25 points	Medium readiness = 15–21 points	Low readiness = 14 points and below

A. "Whatever it takes": To what degree are you willing to do whatever it takes?

Answer the questions below by highlighting your score on the 5-point scale on the right.

	RATING/SCORE		
11. Do you have competing priorities that might demand your attention and detract from your leadership of the change strategy?	**None** (5) 4	**One or two** 3 2	**Several** 1
12. Are you reluctant to label a group as "low readiness"? Are you reluctant to put a lot of structure into your planning and implementation processes?	**Never** (5) 4	**Sometimes** 3 2	**Always** 1
13. Do you believe that you should always treat everyone equally as colleagues regardless of their readiness to participate in the change strategy?	**No** (5) 4	**Somewhat** 3 2	**Yes** 1

Copyright © 2011 by John Wiley & Sons, Inc.

Copyright © 2011 by John Wiley & Sons, Inc.

	RATING/SCORE		
14. Do you consult people whose views may differ from your own?	Always 5　(4)　3	Somewhat 2	Seldom 1
15. Are you open to the resulting plan being different from your original conception (provided that the nonnegotiables are in there)?	Always 5　4	Somewhat (3)　2	Seldom 1

"Whatever it takes" Subtotal: Add your points scored for questions A11–A15. The total point score for "whatever it takes" is _22_ out of 25 possible points. *Therefore, my readiness level regarding "whatever it takes" is (highlight one):* (HIGH) MEDIUM, LOW	High readiness = 22–25 points	Medium readiness 15–21 points	Low readiness = 14 points and below

A. Values: To what degree do you have values that will propel the change process?

Answer the questions below by highlighting your score on the 5-point scale on the right.

16. Do you and the participants have the same definitions/language for the problem to be solved and the methods by which this will be undertaken? Has this assumption been tested?	Definitely 5　4	Perhaps (3)　2	No or don't know 1
17. Are you comfortable with taking risks and learning from mistakes?	Always 5　(4)	Somewhat 3　2	No 1
18. Do you know the values of participants and of the organization and how they may differ from your own?	To a great extent (5)　4	Somewhat 3　2	Not at all 1
19. Do you value flexibility?	Always (5)　4	Somewhat 3　2	Seldom 1
20. Do you model behavior that you want to see as norms, such as adhering to ground rules?	Always (5)　4	Somewhat 3　2	Seldom 1

Values Subtotal: Add your points scored for questions A16–A20. The total point score for "values" is _22_ out of 25 possible points. *Therefore, my readiness level regarding values is (highlight one):* HIGH (MEDIUM), LOW	High readiness= 22–25 points	Medium readiness = 15–21 points	Low readiness = 14 points and below

Section A Summary: Leader's Total Readiness Score (out of 100)

Sub-score for experience:	_19_ out of 25	Readiness level: *Medium*
Sub-score for skills:	_23_ out of 25	Readiness level: *High*
Sub-score for do what it takes	_22_ out of 25	Readiness level: *High*
Sub-score for values:	_22_ out of 25	Readiness level: *High*
TOTAL READINESS SCORE:	_86_ out of 100	
LEADER'S READINESS LEVEL (highlight one): HIGH, MEDIUM, LOW		

High = 88–100; Medium = 87–60; Low = below 60

Copyright © 2011 by John Wiley & Sons, Inc.

SECTION B: PARTICIPANTS' READINESS

> *Readiness = Experience + Skills + Willingness + Shared Values*
>
> *Be candid when completing this tool and try to think of concrete examples when answering the questions. Be careful when noting your ratings; the scale is not the same for all questions.*

Copyright © 2011 by John Wiley & Sons, Inc.

	RATING/SCORE

B. Experience: To what degree do participants have previous experience with change in general and with this type of change in particular?

Answer the questions below by highlighting your score on the 5-point scale on the right.

	All have		Some have		Few have
1. Have participants successfully undergone change in any organization before?	5	4	3	(2)	1
2. Have participants successfully undergone change in *this* organization before?	5	4	3	(2)	1
3. Have participants experienced change in this organization *unsuccessfully*?	5	4	3	(2)	1
4. Do participants have previous successful experience in the content area of the change strategy?	5	(4)	3	2	1

	Definitely		Perhaps		Few will
5. If participants' experience has been negative, are they willing to take a leap of faith now?	5	4	(3)	2	1

	High readiness = 22–25 points	Medium readiness = 15–21 points	Low readiness = 14 points and below
Experience Subtotal: Add your points scored for questions B1–B5. The total point score for "experience" is _13_ out of 25 possible points. *Therefore, participants' readiness level regarding experience is (highlight one):* HIGH, MEDIUM, (LOW)			

B. Required Skills: To what degree do participants have the required skills and knowledge for this change strategy?

Answer the questions below by highlighting your score on the 5-point scale on the right.

	Consistently		Sometimes		Infrequently
6. Have participants demonstrated expertise in the content required by this change strategy?	5	(4)	3	2	1

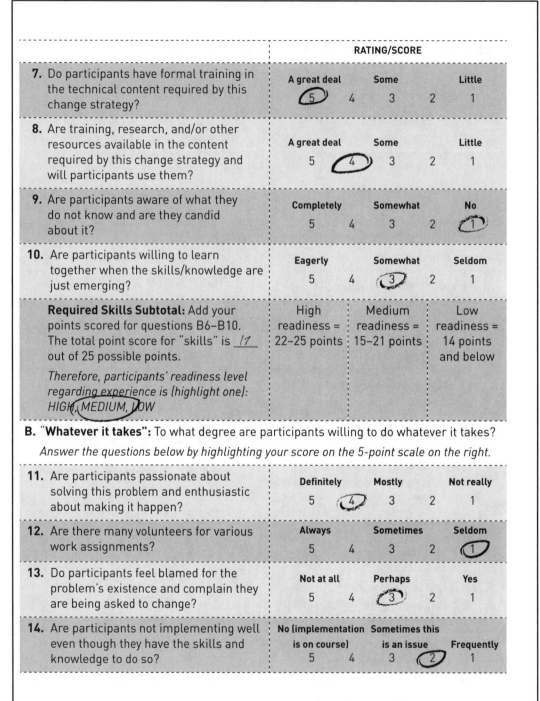

RATING/SCORE				
7. Do participants have formal training in the technical content required by this change strategy?	**A great deal** **(5)**	4	**Some** 3	2	**Little** 1
8. Are training, research, and/or other resources available in the content required by this change strategy and will participants use them?	**A great deal** 5	**(4)**	**Some** 3	2	**Little** 1
9. Are participants aware of what they do not know and are they candid about it?	**Completely** 5	4	**Somewhat** 3	2	**No** **(1)**
10. Are participants willing to learn together when the skills/knowledge are just emerging?	**Eagerly** 5	4	**Somewhat** **(3)**	2	**Seldom** 1

Required Skills Subtotal: Add your points scored for questions B6–B10. The total point score for "skills" is _17_ out of 25 possible points.

Therefore, participants' readiness level regarding experience is (highlight one):
HIGH, (MEDIUM), LOW

High readiness = 22–25 points	Medium readiness = 15–21 points	Low readiness = 14 points and below

B. "Whatever it takes": To what degree are participants willing to do whatever it takes?

Answer the questions below by highlighting your score on the 5-point scale on the right.

11. Are participants passionate about solving this problem and enthusiastic about making it happen?	**Definitely** 5	**(4)**	**Mostly** 3	2	**Not really** 1
12. Are there many volunteers for various work assignments?	**Always** 5	4	**Sometimes** 3	2	**Seldom** **(1)**
13. Do participants feel blamed for the problem's existence and complain they are being asked to change?	**Not at all** 5	4	**Perhaps** **(3)**	2	**Yes** 1
14. Are participants not implementing well even though they have the skills and knowledge to do so?	**No (implementation is on course)** 5	4	**Sometimes this is an issue** 3	**(2)**	**Frequently** 1

Copyright © 2011 by John Wiley & Sons, Inc.

Copyright © 2011 by John Wiley & Sons, Inc.

	RATING/SCORE		
15. Do most people come in early and/or stay until the job is done even if it is past the end of their official day?	Always 5	Sometimes but not the norm 4 3	Seldom (or only one or two reliable people) (2) 1
"Whatever it takes" Subtotal: Add your points scored for questions B11–B15. The total point score for "doing whatever it takes" is _/2_ out of 25 possible points. *Therefore, participants' readiness level regarding doing whatever it takes is (highlight one): HIGH, MEDIUM, LOW*	High readiness = 22–25 points	Medium readiness 15–21 points	Low readiness = 14 points and below

B. Values: To what degree do participants have shared understandings (culture)?

Answer the questions below by highlighting your score on the 5-point scale on the right.

	Always	Sometimes	No or untested
16. Do participants have the same definitions/language for the problem to be solved and the methods by which this will be undertaken? Has this assumption been tested?	5 4	(3) 2	1

	Always	Somewhat	Seldom
17. Are participants comfortable with taking risks and learning from mistakes?	5 4	3 (2)	1
18. Do participants value listening to each other, hearing what each is saying, and testing those assumptions?	5 4	(3) 2	1
19. Are participants comfortable with ambiguity?	5 4	3 2	(1)
20. Do participants value flexibility?	5 4	(3) 2	1

| **Values Subtotal:** Add your points scored for questions B16–B20. The total point score for "shared understandings" is _/2_ out of 25 possible points.

Therefore, participants' readiness level regarding shared understandings is (highlight one): HIGH, MEDIUM, LOW | High readiness= 22–25 points | Medium readiness = 15–21 points | Low readiness = 14 points and below |

Section B Summary: Participants' Total Readiness Scores

Sub-score for experience:	_13_ out of 25	Readiness level: *Low*
Sub-score for skills:	_17_ out of 25	Readiness level: *Medium*
Sub-score for do what it takes	_12_ out of 25	Readiness level: *Low*
Sub-score for values:	_12_ out of 25	Readiness level: *Low*
TOTAL READINESS SCORE:	_54_ out of 100	

LEADER'S READINESS LEVEL (highlight one): HIGH, MEDIUM, ⟨LOW⟩

High = 88–100; Medium = 87–60; Low = 59 and below

Copyright © 2011 by John Wiley & Sons, Inc.

SECTION C: THE ORGANIZATION'S READINESS

> *Readiness = Organizational Experience + Organizational Learning + Organizational Culture + Shared Values About This Change Strategy*
>
> *Be candid when completing this tool and try to think of concrete examples when answering the questions. Be careful when noting your ratings; the scale is not the same for all questions.*

RATING/SCORE

C. Experience: To what degree does the organization have previous experience with change in general and with this type of change in particular?

Answer the questions below by highlighting your score on the 5-point scale on the right.

	RATING/SCORE		
1. Has the organization successfully undergone any type of change before?	**Many times** **Once or twice** **Never** 5 (4) 3 2 1		
2. Has the organization successfully undergone change in the same content area as the proposed change strategy before?	**Many times** **Once or twice** **Never** 5 4 (3) 2 1		
3. Has the organization experienced change in this organization *unsuccessfully*?	**Never** **Once** **More than once** 5 4 (3) 2 1		
4. Does the organization have experience in delivering programs similar in content to those of the change strategy?	**Has all needed expertise** **Has most needed expertise** **Has little needed expertise currently** 5 4 (3) 2 1		
5. If the organization's experience has been negative, does it value risk-taking?	**A great deal** **To a moderate degree** **Seldom** 5 4 3 2 (1)		

Experience Subtotal: Add your points scored for questions C1–C5. The total point score for "experience" is _14_ out of 25 possible points. *Therefore, participants' readiness level regarding experience is (highlight one): HIGH, MEDIUM, LOW*	High readiness = 22–25 points	Medium readiness = 15–21 points	Low readiness = 14 points and below

Copyright © 2011 by John Wiley & Sons, Inc.

	RATING/SCORE

C. Organizational Learning: To what degree does the organization have the capacity to learn the skills that are required for this change strategy?

Answer the questions below by highlighting your score on the 5-point scale on the right.

6. Are there processes in place by which organization members critically reflect on their experiences with their programs (successful and unsuccessful)? If not, will such be put in place for this initiative?	**Definitely** 5	4	**Somewhat** 3	2	**Not at this time** (1)
7. Are there many types of learning taking place (i.e., formal training, informal learning)?	**On-going** 5	(4)	**Some** 3	2	**Little or none** 1
8. Are research, data, and/or other resources available in the content area? Are they valued, used, and discussed?	**Extensive** 5	(4)	**Some** 3	2	**Little or none** 1
9. Is there on-going assessment of each individual's skills versus those needed for his/her role – and a plan for developing skills that need improvement?	**A formal system is in place** 5	4	**Something is done; it might not be formal** (3)	2	**Little or nothing is done** 1
10. Is there a vehicle for learning together when the skills and knowledge are just emerging?	**A formal system is in place** 5	4	**Something is done; it might not be formal** (3)	2	**Little or nothing is done** 1

Organizational Learning Subtotal: Add your points scored for questions C6–C10. The total point score for "skills" is _15_ out of 25 possible points. *Therefore, participants' readiness level regarding experience is (highlight one):* HIGH, MEDIUM, LOW	High readiness = 22–25 points	Medium readiness = 15–21 points	Low readiness = 14 points and below

C. Organizational Culture:

Answer the questions below by highlighting your score on the 5-point scale on the right.

11. Is there a culture of trying to assign blame when things go wrong or a value for being reflective and learning from mistakes?	**No or seldom** 5	4	**To some extent** 3	2	**Yes** (1)
12. Is there a shared value for flexibility? Ambiguity seen as opportunity?	**Always** 5	4	**Sometimes** 3	(2)	**Seldom** 1

Copyright © 2011 by John Wiley & Sons, Inc.

Copyright © 2011 by John Wiley & Sons, Inc.

	RATING/SCORE		
13. Is there a culture of mutual respect? Is listening to each other valued?	**Always** 5 4	**Sometimes** (3) 2	**Seldom** 1
14. Is there a strong organizational work ethic?	**Always** 5 4	**Sometimes** (3) 2	**Seldom** 1
15. Are there rituals or ceremonies to celebrate successes?	**Always** 5 4	**Sometimes** (3) 2	**Seldom** 1
Organizational culture Subtotal: Add your points scored for questions C11–C15. The total point score for "organizational culture" is _12_ out of 25 possible points. *Therefore, participants' readiness level regarding doing whatever it takes is* (highlight one): HIGH, MEDIUM, **LOW**	High readiness = 22–25 points	Medium readiness 15–21 points	Low readiness = 14 points and below

C. Shared Values: Shared values about the change strategy?

Answer the questions below by highlighting your score on the 5-point scale on the right.

	RATING/SCORE		
16. Are the terms in use for the change strategy commonly understood? Has this assumption been tested?	**Yes** 5 4	**Perhaps** 3 (2)	**No** 1
17. Are there shared norms of behavior (such as ground rules and agendas for meetings as a matter of course)?	**Yes** 5 4	**Somewhat** (3) 2	**No** 1
18. Is there a shared value for the importance of the problem being addressed by the change strategy?	**Yes** 5 4	**Somewhat** (3) 2	**No** 1
19. Is there a shared belief that this change strategy will help solve the problem?	**Yes** 5 4	**Somewhat** 3 (2)	**No** 1
20. Is there a shared belief that this change strategy will be successfully implemented?	**Yes** 5 4	**Somewhat** 3 2	**No** (1)
Shared Values Subtotal: Add your points scored for questions C16–C20. The total point score for "shared values" is _11_ out of 25 possible points. *Therefore, participants' readiness level regarding shared understandings is* (highlight one): HIGH, MEDIUM, **LOW**	High readiness= 22–25 points	Medium readiness = 15–21 points	Low readiness = 14 points and below

Section C Summary: Organization's Total Readiness Score (out of 100)

Sub-score for experience:	_14_ out of 25	Readiness level: *Low*
Sub-score for organizational learning:	_15_ out of 25	Readiness level: *Low*
Sub-score for organizational culture:	_12_ out of 25	Readiness level: *Low*
Sub-score for shared values:	_11_ out of 25	Readiness level: *Low*
TOTAL READINESS SCORE:	_52_ out of 100	
LEADER'S READINESS LEVEL (highlight one): HIGH, MEDIUM, ~~LOW~~		

High = 88–100; Medium = 87–60; Low = 59 and below

TOTAL READINESS RECAP (TRANSCRIBE FROM YOUR TOTALS FROM SECTIONS A, B, AND C)

Leader's readiness level is (highlight one):	HIGH MEDIUM LOW
Participants' readiness is (highlight one):	HIGH MEDIUM LOW
Organization's readiness is (highlight one):	HIGH MEDIUM LOW

■ ■ ■

Determining Strategies to Accommodate and Improve Existing Readiness (of the Leader, the Participants, and the Organization)

- *What is the readiness of the leader? Of the participants? Of the organization?*

- *What are specific areas of high and low readiness for each? How will you accommodate them in your plans?*

- *Where are the gaps between participants and leader? Participants and organization? Leader and organization?*

- *What will you do to address those gaps?*

- *What type of structure will you build into your implementation plans? Which methods and how?*

Copyright © 2011 by John Wiley & Sons, Inc.

Strategies I Might Try as a Result of This Analysis

1. For the leader: *Develop methods to persuade participants to "unfreeze" their previous negative experience with change. Perhaps an "early win" might help.*

2. For the participants: *Role model commitment to the project (come in early; stay late); survey participants regarding why implementation is not happening well even though they have the skills; involve participants in collaborative planning that is highly structured.*

3. For the organization: *Develop highly structured processes by which organization members can learn from their collective experiences in a nonthreatening manner; develop and publicize ground rules for all meetings; celebrate successes with ceremonies; create new rituals such as weekly success-sharing meetings.*

Copyright © 2011 by John Wiley & Sons, Inc.

RESISTANCE REDUCER

Change Strategy Under Consideration: *HHS Teacher Training System Reform*

_____

_____

Note that many of the forms in this book can be downloaded for free from the Jossey-Bass Web site. Go to: www.josseybass.com/go/spiro.

> **Effective Resistance Management = Preventing + Reducing + Tolerating**
>
> *Be candid when completing this tool and try to think of concrete examples when answering the questions. Be careful when noting your ratings; the scale descriptions are not the same for all questions.*

■ ■ ■

	RATING/SCORE

A. Preventing Resistance: To what degree can you prevent resistance before you start?

Answer the questions below by highlighting your score on the 5-point scale on the right.

1. Participants' readiness has been analyzed and activities are matched with that. Provision has been made to reanalyze to make midcourse corrections.	To a great extent Somewhat Not at all (5) 4 3 2 1
2. It is recognized that people have different attitudes about change and ways of dealing with it. An effort is made to find out how the individual participants feel about change and develop strategies to make each feel comfortable. Surveys, interviews, and focus groups are used to gather information.	To a great extent Somewhat Not at all 5 4 (3) 2 1
3. There are many other changes going on at the same time as this one.	Not at all Somewhat To a large extent 5 4 3 (2) 1
4. Advantages and disadvantages of the change strategy from *participants'* points of view are identified up front. Strategies are developed to increase participants' perceived benefits and to decrease the negatives. The leader accepts that participants may buy into the change for reasons other than those that motivate the leader.	To a great extent Somewhat Not at all 5 4 3 (2) 1

Copyright © 2011 by John Wiley & Sons, Inc.

RATING/SCORE

5. When communicating about the change strategy, the leader considers what people will hear as opposed to what he or she *thinks* is being said.

To a great extent		Somewhat		Not at all
5	4	3	2	(1)

6. Participants feel blamed for the need to have change. If they had done their work better, change would not be necessary.

Not at all		Somewhat		To a great extent
5	4	3	(2)	1

7. The leader is an active listener. He or she can turn off his or her own opinions and really hear others. The leader paraphrases the speaker often to confirm understanding.

To a great extent		Somewhat		Not at all
5	4	(3)	2	1

Resistance Prevention Subtotal: Add your points scored for questions A1–A7. The total point score for "resistance prevention" is _19_ out of 35 possible points.

The resistance prevention level is (highlight one): HIGH, MEDIUM, (LOW)

High resistance prevention = 32–35 points	Medium resistance prevention = 21–31 points	Low resistance prevention = (20 points and below)

B. Minimizing Resistance: To what degree can you reduce resistance as you go along?

Answer the questions below by highlighting your score on the 5-point scale on the right.

1. There is awareness that resistance comes with the territory in leading change, because participants are likely to experience loss and anxiety. Attempts are made to spot resistance at its earliest stages.

To a great extent		Somewhat		Not at all
5	(4)	3	2	1

2. If some participants agree with the change in public—but talk against it in private—an effort is made to understand and address their points of view.

To a great extent		Somewhat		Not at all
5	4	3	(2)	1

3. Resisters are engaged in collaborative planning for the change strategy, often teaming them with others who are genuine supporters of the change strategy.

To a great extent		Somewhat		Not at all
5	4	(3)	2	1

Copyright © 2011 by John Wiley & Sons, Inc.

Copyright © 2011 by John Wiley & Sons, Inc.

	RATING/SCORE		
4. If the organization values competition, such tactics are used to motivate, but if there is no such value, competition is not encouraged.	**To a great extent** 5 4 ③	**Somewhat** 2	**Not at all** 1
5. Successes are celebrated with ceremonies and new rituals.	**To a great extent** 5 ④ 3	**Somewhat** 2	**Not at all** 1
6. Learning is deliberately incorporated in most activities (even if it is informal or networking).	**To a great extent** 5 ④ 3	**Somewhat** 2	**Not at all** 1
7. Participants believe that they are being treated fairly. For example: "negative balance of consequences"—whereby people who do the best job are "rewarded" by getting more to do without additional compensation—is avoided.	**To a great extent** 5 4 3	**Somewhat** ②	**Not at all** 1
Resistance Reducing Subtotal: Add your points scored for questions B1–B7. The total point score for "reducing resistance" is _22_ out of 35 possible points. *The reducing resistance score is: (highlight one): HIGH, MEDIUM, LOW*	High Resistance Reduction = 32–35 points	Medium Resistance Reduction = 21–31 points	Low Resistance Reduction = 20 points or below

C. Tolerating Resistance

For the leader: To what degree can you tolerate resistance when it cannot be prevented or minimized?

Answer the questions below by highlighting your score on the 5-point scale on the right.

1. I am totally committed to the change strategy and believe strongly that it will be beneficial. Therefore, I am willing to encounter whatever resistance I cannot prevent or mimimize.	**To a great extent** ⑤ 4	**Somewhat** 3 2	**Not at all** 1
2. I analyze the political power of those who are resisting to determine if they represent larger constituencies as opposed to individual issues. If resisters are individuals, I am prepared to tolerate their opposition.	**To a great extent** 5 4	**Somewhat** 3 ②	**Not at all** 1

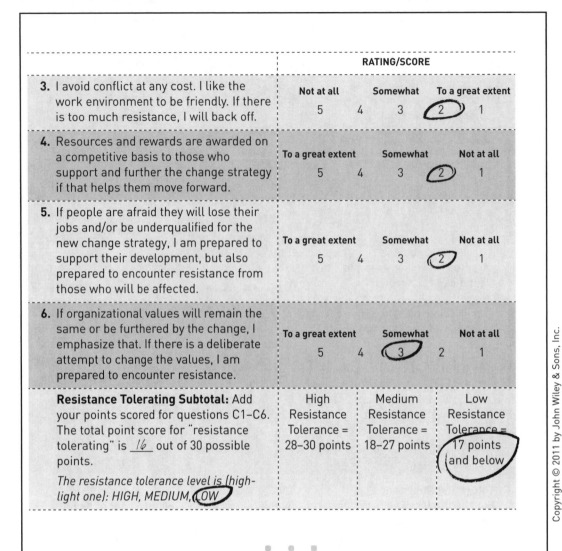

	RATING/SCORE		
3. I avoid conflict at any cost. I like the work environment to be friendly. If there is too much resistance, I will back off.	Not at all 5	Somewhat 4 3	To a great extent (2) 1
4. Resources and rewards are awarded on a competitive basis to those who support and further the change strategy if that helps them move forward.	To a great extent 5	Somewhat 4 3	Not at all (2) 1
5. If people are afraid they will lose their jobs and/or be underqualified for the new change strategy, I am prepared to support their development, but also prepared to encounter resistance from those who will be affected.	To a great extent 5	Somewhat 4 3	Not at all (2) 1
6. If organizational values will remain the same or be furthered by the change, I emphasize that. If there is a deliberate attempt to change the values, I am prepared to encounter resistance.	To a great extent 5	Somewhat 4 (3)	Not at all 2 1
Resistance Tolerating Subtotal: Add your points scored for questions C1–C6. The total point score for "resistance tolerating" is _16_ out of 30 possible points. *The resistance tolerance level is (highlight one): HIGH, MEDIUM, (LOW)*	High Resistance Tolerance = 28–30 points	Medium Resistance Tolerance = 18–27 points	Low Resistance Tolerance = (17 points and below)

Copyright © 2011 by John Wiley & Sons, Inc.

●   ●   ■

Tips for interpreting your results:

- If you are in the medium category, you might go further to see if you are "high" medium or "low" medium. If you are in the "low-medium" range, you might consider yourself "low" as you plan your resistance strategies.

- If you score "3" or below on any statement, you might consider developing a resistance strategy. You should prioritize having strategies for any 1s, 2s, or 3s.

- On resistance tolerance, the following definitions might be useful: high means that the leader is willing to do whatever it takes to achieve the change strategy; medium means that the leader prefers little resistance, but is willing to encounter some in order to achieve the strategy; and low means that the leader wants a conflict-free environment and will not pursue a change strategy that encounters any serious resistance.

- A "low" rating for resistance tolerance for a given change strategy might cause you to reconsider pursuing that work.

Total Resistance Recap
(Transcribe from Your Totals from Sections A, B, and C)

A. Sub-score for resistance prevention:	_18_ out of 35	Level: Low
B. Sub-score for resistance reducing:	_22_ out of 35	Level: Medium
C. Sub-score for resistance tolerance:	_16_ out of 30	Level: Low
TOTAL RESISTANCE REDUCER SCORE:	_56_ out of 100	Level: Low

High = 92–100; Medium = 60–91; Low = 57 and below

■ ■ ■

Implications for Going Forward

A. Resistance prevention strategies I might consider:

1. *Analyze advantages and disadvantages of the strategy from participants' point of view.*

2. *When communicating, consider what others will hear as opposed to what I think I am saying (list out: when I say X, what are people likely to hear)?*

3. *Be sensitive that people hear the need for change as blaming and do not perpetuate that in my communications.*

B. Resistance reducing strategies I might consider:

1. *Analyze where there might be unfair workloads and either even them out or provide extra compensation for those who are carrying a heavier load.*

Copyright © 2011 by John Wiley & Sons, Inc.

2. *Rethink the competitive process for deciding who gets to partici-pate in outside workshops. If this isn't an organizational value, it might be fueling resistance.*

3. *Jim and Sally often are critical in private although they are supportive in public. Meet with them each privately and try to find out their concerns.*

C. Resistance tolerance strategies I might consider:

1. *Be prepared to make hard decisions. Decide how much discomfort I am willing to feel in order to get this done. How committed am I?*

2. *Analyze the power positions of the main resisters and, if they are outliers, be prepared to encounter resistance from them.*

3. *Set priorities and accomplish them despite resistance. Use those ac-complishments to minimize resistance in the future. Use early wins.*

Copyright © 2011 by John Wiley & Sons, Inc.

SCALE AND SUSTAINABILITY SCORE SHEET

Be candid when answering these questions and try to think of evidence to support your ratings.

Note that many of the forms in this book can be downloaded for free from the Jossey-Bass Web site. Go to: www.josseybass.com/go/spiro.

Step 1: Assess the Leader's Readiness to Plan and Implement Scale and Sustainability

- Am I willing to identify the several program elements as core or non-negotiable?

- Am I willing to let go of the notion that every part of the program is essential, and encourage adaptation of the noncore elements based on local needs?

- Can I make the hard choices to reallocate current resources to the scale and sustainability of the current program (if it is a higher priority)?

- Am I prepared to be opportunistic? Am I willing to revise and adapt the plan when circumstances change?

Step 2: Describe the Program or Practice Resulting from Your Change Strategy That You Are Considering Scaling and Sustaining

What is it? Why is it important? How do you know it is of high quality and valued? What results are anticipated? How might behavior change in the long run?

Teachers across the country will be using new pedagogies that facilitate students' "critical thinking" as opposed to rote learning.

Copyright © 2011 by John Wiley & Sons, Inc.

Step 3: List the Core or Nonnegotiable Elements of the Program or Practice

1. A corps of national trainers who will be able to train regional and local trainers

2. A set of curriculum guides for teacher trainers in the 6 main content areas: active learning pedagogies, differentiating instruction, conflict resolution, economic education, technology, and classroom management

3. A central repository for materials as they are developed

4. A group of expert consultants to train the trainers and help in the development of the curriculum guides

5. The support of the Ministry of Education for making the teacher trainer position officially recognized and compensated and dissemination of trainer's guides

Copyright © 2011 by John Wiley & Sons, Inc.

Step 4: Scale

To what extent have the following elements been incorporated into your program or practice?

FOR PLANNING (P)		FOR IMPLEMENTATION (I)	
5 =	A comprehensive plan in place that all stakeholders "own"	5 =	All aspects have been fully implemented
4 =	A comprehensive plan in place that most stakeholders support	4 =	Most aspects have been fully implemented
3 =	A plan in place with some support	3 =	Some aspects have been implemented
2 =	A partial plan with modest support	2 =	Few aspects have been implemented
1 =	No plan	1 =	No aspects have been implemented

	SCALE CATEGORY	(P)	(I)	TOTAL P + I	WHAT MORE IS NEEDED FOR SCALE?
				RATINGS	
I.	A model with demonstrated effectiveness or promise	5	5	10	N/A
II.	A program or practice not only in more places, but with high quality and depth of implementation in all those places	5	2	7	Quality implementation in more places
III.	An underlying set of principles with action steps leading to the model's desired outcomes	5	5	10	N/A
IV.	A justified hypothesis and/or research that supports the rationale behind the model	5	1	6	More buy-in for the research and hypothesis by those who will be implementing in new places

Copyright © 2011 by John Wiley & Sons, Inc.

	SCALE CATEGORY	RATINGS			
		(P)	(I)	TOTAL P + I	WHAT MORE IS NEEDED FOR SCALE?
V.	Replication of identified core elements of the original model with contextual modifications; ownership by local adapters	5	4	9	N/A
VI.	High demand; fills an acknowledged need; market has been demonstrated	3	2	5	More acknowledgment of local need versus need expressed by the Ministry of Education (which is clearly there)
VII.	A large number of supporters beyond those first to embrace the strategy	3	1	4	Needs more buy-in from the next level of implementers
VIII.	Structures or mechanisms through which the model can be spread	5	2	7	The government structures exist under the Ministry of Education. Need more support from universities and nongovernmental sectors. Also, need to get further assurance from the ministry that they won't back out.
IX.	Personnel who are skilled in the model and can train others	5	5	10	N/A
X.	A detailed implementation plan with monitoring and continuous improvement built in	5	2	7	The plan is there. The implementation of the plan will be difficult.
	SCALE Total (P & I) out of 100 →	46	29	75	
	Total	(P)	(I)	(P+I)	

Copyright © 2011 by John Wiley & Sons, Inc.

Step 5: Sustainability

To what extent have the following elements been incorporated into your program or practice?

FOR PLANNING (P)	FOR IMPLEMENTATION (I)
5 = A comprehensive plan in place that all stakeholders "own"	5 = All aspects have been fully implemented
4 = A comprehensive plan in place that most stakeholders support	4 = Most aspects have been fully implemented
3 = A plan in place with some support	3 = Some aspects have been implemented
2 = A partial plan with modest support	2 = Few aspects have been implemented
1 = No plan	1 = No aspects have been implemented

	SUSTAINABILITY ELEMENT	(P)	(I)	TOTAL P + I	WHAT MORE IS NEEDED FOR SUSTAINABILITY?
I. LAWS, REGULATIONS, POLICIES					
a.	Supportive laws or regulations in place	5	0	5	Need new national laws establishing the position of teacher trainer; it is planned, but not implemented.
b.	Institutionalized outcomes of the change (i.e., procedures, position descriptions, curriculum requirements)	5	3	8	The Ministry of Education has promulgated regulations with new training.
	I. AVERAGE SCORES FOR CATEGORY	5	1.5	6.5	
II. KEY INDIVIDUALS					
a.	Key stakeholders engaged	5	4	9	
b.	Little active opposition	2	2	4	There is a good deal of opposition. Need to engage the executive directors of the national education association and the society for curriculum development, both of which are important organizations currently left out.

Copyright © 2011 by John Wiley & Sons, Inc.

SUSTAINABILITY ELEMENT	(P)	(I)	TOTAL P + I	WHAT MORE IS NEEDED FOR SUSTAINABILITY?
II. AVERAGE SCORES FOR CATEGORY	3.5	3	6.5	
III. EXTERNAL PARTNERSHIPS				
a. Key organizations engaged	2	2	4	*Get more participants from universities.*
b. Key organizations perceive the program or practice as furthering their own goals	4	3	7	*Survey for nonparticipating organizations, particularly at the local level, that should be engaged.*
c. Union contracts support the program or practice	N/A	N/A	N/A	
III. AVERAGE SCORES FOR CATEGORY	3.5	2.5	6.0	
IV. INTERNAL ORGANIZATIONAL CAPACITY				
a. Organizational goals furthered by the change	5	5	10	*Ministry's goals and country's goals furthered*
b. Well-defined procedures and systems for implementation	4	4	8	*Ministry has well-defined procedures.*
IV. AVERAGE SCORES FOR CATEGORY	4.5	4.5	9	
V. HUMAN CAPITAL				
a. A clear and legitimate procedure of succession for those leading the effort	0	0	0	*Need succession planning*
b. Mechanisms are in place to ensure that transitions to new staff are as seamless as possible	2	2	4	*Need to document all key processes and decisions; collaborative planning materials will help*
c. Staff with the skills and knowledge to implement the new program or practice	4	5	9	*Need to train more locally*
d. An institutionalized system for training personnel in the skills needed by the program or practice, including training the next generation of change leaders for this initiative	3	3	6	*Need a more formalized system and need to involve the universities*

Copyright © 2011 by John Wiley & Sons, Inc.

SUSTAINABILITY ELEMENT	(P)	(I)	TOTAL P + I	WHAT MORE IS NEEDED FOR SUSTAINABILITY?
V. AVERAGE SCORES FOR CATEGORY	2.3	2.5	4.8	
VI. FUNDING				
a. Ongoing funding from diversified sources (no reliance on a single source of funding)	3	3	6	*Funding is assured, but it is at too low a level; dependent on government funding; need to develop new funding sources and fund at a more appropriate level*
b. Distinction between what is essential from what is *desirable*; and full, ongoing funding for all essentials is in place	3	3	6	*Distinguish further among the essentials and shift funding to these*
c. Reallocation of resources to the new program or practice including cutting funding to programs that are not working well	3	3	6	*Ensure funding for printing/ distributing teacher's guides even if funds are cut from someplace else.*
d. The "real" costs of the program are identified. It is known what the program actually costs when the core elements are fully implemented	2	2	4	*A cost analysis should be done.*
e. The new program is incorporated into existing programs and thereby leverages the funding from the existing programs so no new funding is required	5	5	10	*N/A*
VI. AVERAGE SCORES FOR CATEGORY	3.2	3.2	6.4	
VII. CULTURE				
a. Program or practice furthers existing values and norms	2	2	4	*The value needs to be proven.*
b. Favorable attitudes toward the new program or practice	3	3	6	*Interview teachers to determine barriers*

Copyright © 2011 by John Wiley & Sons, Inc.

SUSTAINABILITY ELEMENT	(P)	(I)	TOTAL P + I	WHAT MORE IS NEEDED FOR SUSTAINABILITY?
VII. AVERAGE SCORES FOR CATEGORY	2.5	2.5	5	
VIII. CONTINUOUS IMPROVEMENT				
a. Continuous gathering of data to support the achievement of the change goal	4	4	8	N/A
b. Provisions for monitoring, learning lessons, and consequently making midcourse corrections	4	4	8	N/A
VIII. AVERAGE SCORES FOR CATEGORY	4	4	8	N/A
IX. COMMUNICATIONS				
a. Ongoing communications mechanisms including use of media and public relations	4	4	8	N/A
b. Transparency of progress to all constituencies	3	3	6	More transparency! Newsletters, press conferences
IX. AVERAGE SCORES FOR CATEGORY	3.5	3.5	7	
X. EVALUATION (SUMMATIVE)				
a. Assessment of the program's or practice's accomplishments versus planned outcomes after a specified time period; identified lessons learned	5	5	10	N/A
X. AVERAGE SCORES FOR CATEGORY	5	5	10	N/A
SUSTAINABILITY GRAND TOTAL → Total the Averages (Out of 100)	31	32.2	69.2	
Total	(P)	(I)	(P+I)	

Copyright © 2011 by John Wiley & Sons, Inc.

Copyright © 2011 by John Wiley & Sons, Inc.

Step 6: Determining Strategies for Scaling and Sustaining the Results of the Change Strategy

You will have a rating for each scale and sustainability element. This should enable you to ask the following questions:

1. *What more do I need to plan to get scale (in order of importance)?*

   - *Supporters beyond those already engaged*
   - *Greater acknowledgment that there is a need for different teaching methodologies to be used in schools across the country*

2. *What more do I need to implement to get scale (in order of importance)?*

   - *Evidence of quality implementation in more places*
   - *More supporters beyond those already engaged*
   - *Structures or mechanisms through which the training can spread*
   - *A detailed implementation plan that includes all the above*

3. *What more do I need to plan for sustainability (in order of importance)?*

   - *Succession planning for key positions*
   - *Engage the executive directors of the national education association and the society for curriculum development in Pacifica (prove the value of the program)*
   - *An institutionalized system for training teachers*
   - *Determining the "real" cost of this program*

4. *What more do I need to do for sustainability (in order of importance)?*

   - *Laws that support the implementation of this strategy (such as a formal teacher trainer position)*
   - *Succession planning for key positions*
   - *An institutionalized system for training teachers*
   - *Need to engage the executive directors of the national education association and the society for curriculum development in Pacifica (prove the value of the program)*
   - *Determining the "real" cost of this program*

Index

Changeville Public School District (hypothetical organization), 9, 15, 44; and assessing readiness for new leader changing program, 47–48; and assessment of resistance for new core curriculum, 86–87; and Changeville Board of Education, 66; and Changeville Board of Education analysis of stakeholders for development of core curriculum in mathematics, 66–67; and Changeville High Schools reworking of class rosters in middle of school year, 156–157; collaborative planning process to decrease student dropout rate at, 119–122; and development of core curriculum in third-grade mathematics, 98–99; dropout prevention program at, 144; and focus on programs and services for highest-needs schools, 21; mathematics curriculum, 144

Collaboration: achieving, without disintegration, 101–122; determining strategies for, 113; and using collaborative planning parameters, 113–117

Collaborative planning parameters, 108; action planning sheet for, 113–117; and assumptions of what has been decided, 116; and atmosphere of respect, 116; determining strategies for, 113; and high structure and clarity/transparency, 115; and integration of learning, 116–117; leader's self-reflection questions for, 109; and mandates, constraints, and nonnegotiables, 116; and presentation of results of pre-work survey, 115; and readiness assessment/structure of meeting, 115; and right participants, 115; and use of writing for focus and structure, 115–116

Core elements, 131

Course corrections, 6

Culture: change in, 126–130; program embedded in, 126

D

Data, use of, 151–152

Destination, *versus* journey, 9–10

Details, 150–151

Determining change strategy (Step one), 5, 13–22, 141; common mistakes to avoid in, 17–18; essential elements for, 13–17; and making plan, 13–22; and mission statement, 14; scaling and sustaining in, 6; strategy/action aligner for, 18–20; tactics for, 13–18; tool for, 18–20

E

Early win wonder tool, 94–97

Engaging key players in planning (Step Six), 101–122; and achieving collaboration without disintegration, 101–122; action planning sheet for, 113–117; and collaborative planning parameters, 108–112; common mistakes to avoid in, 105–108; and diversity of perspective, 104; essential elements for, 103–105; leader's self-reflective questions for, 109; tactics for, 103–108

F

Field-tested tools, 6–8

Funding, 132

G

General style, 161

of sustainability, 125–126; and determining strategies for scaling and sustaining results of change strategy, 141, 195; essential elements in, 127–130; and management of staff turnover and transitions, 130; real goal of, 126–130; scoresheet tool for, 133–140, 187–195; and sustainable training program for principals, 130–131; tactics for, 125–133

Securing small early win (Step Five), 6, 89–99; common mistakes to avoid in, 93–94; determining strategies for, 97; and early win wonder tool, 94–97; essential elements for, 91–92; and examples of early wins, 92–93; leader's self-reflection questions for, 95; tactics for, 91–94

Staff turnovers, 130

Stakeholders. *See* Analyzing stakeholders (Step Three)

State Board of Education, 55

Strategies: distinguishing, from action, 16–17; identifying potentially most effective, 15–17

Strategy/Action Aligner, 18–20, 91

Struggle, tales of, 8–9

Suburban school districts, 56

Success, tales of, 8–9

Sustainability, 125–126; equating, with funding, 132; *versus* funding, 132; *versus* self-perpetuating, 132–133

T

Tactics: common mistakes to avoid in, 17–18; and distinguishing strategy from action, 16–17; and essential elements, 13–17; and essential elements and mistakes to avoid, 6; and identifying potentially most effective strategies, 15–17; and internal negotiations of mission statement, 14; and mission statement, 14; successful use of, 159–163; and tools, 7

Talent Unlimited Inc. (TUI; hypothetical organization), 9, 29; and expansion of services to other cities, which have adapted and sustained them, 143; analysis of stakeholders in potential expansion to other cities, 66; and assessing readiness to participate in virtual professional learning community, 45–47; and change of content in early win strategy, 156; and collaborative planning process with potential users of product, 118–119; decision of, on high level strategy, 16–17; and decision to hold statewide conference, 98; and expanding use of products and services to nonprofit organizations in other cities, 21; mission statement of, 15; plans of, for resistance from staff members of potential client organizations, 85–86

Teacher trainers, 155

Teacher unions, 56

Three R's tool, 153–154

Time coach, 129

Tools, successful use of, 159–163

Transitions, 130

Trust, 107–108

Turnaround School, 9; and analysis of stakeholders for developing new lesson plans in mathematics, 67; and assessing readiness for developing new lessons plan, 48; and change in main action by principal, 157; collaborative planning at, 122; and first meeting of new professional learning community, 99; functioning leadership team and ongoing professional learning community at, 144-145; and involving school community in developing new ways to engage students in learning, 22; mission statement of, 15; plans of, for resistance to

new professional learning community (PLC), 87; statewide conference at, 98

U

Universities, 56

Urban school districts, 56

W

Web site, 93